1. INTRODUCTION

The Roman army during the Second Punic War, a citizen army, developed also in parallel a professional army, the *legiones cannenses* or the Cannae's legions, formed by the veterans of the battle of Cannae (216 BCE). These units showed the same characteristics of the Late Republic and Imperial Roman army already one hundred years before the reforms of Marius. But, how and why a citizen's army became a professional force?

There are three main reasons that could explain the transformation of a citizen's army in a professional force, the split of the legionaries from civic life, consequence of the *Senatus Consultum* of 215 BCE, which stripped the common soldiers of their civic rights, the peculiar commitment and loyalty to each of the warlords, that the *legiones cannenses* served, namely Marcus Claudius Marcellus, the conqueror of Syracuse, Publius Cornelius Scipio Africanus, who defeated Hannibal at the battle of Zama, and, last but not least, Titus Quinctius Flamininus, who beat the Macedonian phalanx at the battle of Cynoscephalae, and the evolution and changing of the tactical composition of the legions, from the *manipular* legion, identical to the other contemporary units, to units which emphasized the primary importance of the *cohors* and the *centuria*, as in the late Republican and early Imperial legions.

Once, is made clear the peculiarity of the *legiones cannenses*, I shall proceed to a narration of the history, or more exactly, the *Histories* of these units, from the formation of its earlier units, probably as early as 218 BCE, when the first two legions were levied, till their definitive disbandment in the wake of the Second Macedonian War. Thrice, I let the sources speak by themselves, first in the description of the battle of Cannae, and then, the successive encounters of Zama and Cynoscephalae, the three main battles, in which the *legiones cannenses* took part.

INDEX

▲ **Roman Republic Coins minted during the Second Punic War**
Stater, *Gold, minted in Rome, 225-212 BCE; Obverse: Laureate, Janiform head of Dioscuri. Border of dots. Reverse: Oath-taking scene. Two soldiers facing each other, one bearded and without armor, one beardless and in armor; each holds spear in left hand and with sword in right hand touches pig held by figure kneeling between them; in exergue, inscription: ROMA*

2. THE SPLIT OF THE LEGIONARIES FROM CIVIC LIFE - THE ROMAN CITIZEN SOLDIER BECOMES A PROFESSIONAL SOLDIER

The common soldier in the Roman army was a citizen. Thus, the Roman army was composed by citizen soldiers. The Roman citizens serving in these legions, accomplished their legal obligations towards the state. Each Roman citizen was obliged to serve for sixteen years, although, according to Pthe Second Punic War, citizens could serve for no less than twenty years. After the accomplishment of sixteen years of military service, a citizen is considered emeritus. Equites, however, served only for ten years (Polybius, *Histories* VI, 19).

Romans served as *iuniores* between the age of 17 till the age of 46, and from the age of 46 till the age of 60 years old as *seniores*. After the age of 60, Roman citizens were exonerated from military service (Varro, *Nonius*, 523, 24).

Each year, once the Senate passed the relative decree to decide how many men must be levied, the two consuls began the *dilectus* (in Latin selection) or levy. In the period considered each year were generally levied four legions, two for each consul. According to Polybius (Polybius, Histories VI, 19-20), first of all, the consuls appoint all the 24 tribunes, of whom 14 already had seen five years of military service and 10 had seen already ten years of service. The *dilectus* itself began when a red flag was raised on the Capitol to indicate the beginning of the levy (Festus 92 L). All the citizens were called up divided according to tribe, but only some (enough for the four legions) were selected according to lots. The 14 younger *tribunes* thus called the names of the citizens selected by lot and divided them in four groups as the four legions. First the tribunes are assigned to the legions.

After the levy, all the citizens took the oath of allegiance. The tribunes select a man for each legion. He took the oath, administered by the tribunes, and the other soldiers answer "Idem in me". This oath was symbolic because it represented for the citizen the transition between the civic environment with its laws and the military discipline, to which he was now subjected. At the same time that the *dilectus* was performed in Rome, the consuls send orders to the magistrates of allied cities in Italy from where they wish to raise troops, stating the number required and day and place where selected men must appear. The local authorities administer the oath (Polybius, *Histories* VI, 21).[1]

Thus, the soldiers that would form the *legiones cannenses* were citizens similar to all the other citizens that served in the other legions levied by the Republic. Once in the army, the relationship of the soldiers with the Roman state was modified by the needs of military discipline. The Roman citizens had a well-defined relationship with the state, which was governed through the exercise of their duties and rights, even if these differed according to the social status of the citizen. However, once the Roman citizens became soldiers and part of the army, their civic rights were now altered by the needs of military discipline. Thus, in this process their civic identity shifted from that of individuals, each part of a social class, to that of a collective body, the Roman legion, whose internal framework differed from those, which they habitually confronted as citizens. This can explain why the Senate, in the wake of the defeat of Cannae, behaved towards the soldiers in the same way as they perceived, once under arms, as a collective body.

It is very important to emphasize that the oath of allegiance to the Roman Republic mirrored the most basic ideal of ancient Rome, that of *fides* (Livy, *Roman History* I.32). The concept of *fides* can be roughly translated with the idea of good faith or trust. *Fides* as mutual trust stood at the foundation of the Roman state. Any transactions among the Romans, and between the Romans and their neighbors, was always under the aegis of *fides*. Once the Romans made an agreement, characterized by *fides*, this

---

1   See C. Nicolet, *Le métier de citoyen dans la Rome républicaine*, Paris 1976, pp. 133-140. See also P. Connolly, *Greece and Rome at War*, London 1981, p. 129.

1

2

means that the Roman Republic was acting following what was *fas*, i.e., that was right in the eyes of the gods. Once the other side broke the agreement, in fact they did not just broke the *fides* or trust, but did something *nefas*, or unjust in the eyes of the gods. Therefore, the Romans resorted to war as their last choice, to uphold the broken *fides*, and to rebuild what is *fas*, or right in the eyes of the gods.[2] When the Roman citizen soldiers and the army of their allies, or *socii*, were defeated at Cannae, they broke the *fides* they owned through the oath of allegiance to the Roman Republic. Once, in the eyes of the Roman Senate, the soldiers that took part in the battle of Cannae were defeated with ignominy, thus, they had broken the trust between them and the Roman Republic. These soldiers, therefore, could not be trusted anymore. As they had broken with their behavior the *fides* that bonded them to the Roman state, they had to be punished. From the moment they had broken the trust, every action they took was *nefas*. They were, by now, beyond the reach of human law.

Usually legionary soldiers were punished each for his own misdemeanor, sometimes harshly with fustigation. However, collective punishment as decimation did exist. Still a Roman legion, as a gathering of individuals, even if misbehaved, was never totally divorced and cast out from the society. On the contrary, even after a punishment, individual or collective, these soldiers remained members of the surrounding civil society because they were both citizens and soldiers. Thus, the fact that these citizens, now soldiers and members of a collective body, were collectively punished, because as members of a collective body, the legion, they had broken their mutual engagement of *fides*, or trust towards the Roman state is nothing unusual in the history of the Roman Republic. But how these soldiers were punished?

The *senatus consultum* hold in 215 BCE can be reconstructed from indirect evidence. In the year 212 BCE, when Marcellus was in Sicily, one of the soldiers of the *legiones cannenses* sent him a letter, in which he begs to take parts in the military operations in Sicily, together with his comrades (Livy, *History of Rome* XXV, 5). From this letter it is possible to reconstruct the *senatus consultum* hold

---

2   Some modern historians, such as Maurice Holleaux, accepts Livy's concept of *fides*, as standing behind the foreign policy of the Roman Republic, and therefore that the Romans always reacted, not acted, that their foreign policy developed under their enemies' coercion and constraint, and that, whenever possible, the Romans always tried to go back on their conquests. This thesis had been lately proposed once more by Gruen. On the other hand, other historians, such as Robert Harris, argue that the Roman Republic aimed from the beginning at conquest and developed an articulated imperialist policy of war and intervention. See E.S. Gruen, "Polybius and Josephus on Rome"," in J. Pastor, P. Stern, M. Mor (eds.), *Flavius Josephus, Interpretation and History, Supplements to the Journal for the Study of Judaism* 146, Leiden 2011, pp. 149-162. See also W. Harris, *War and Imperialism in Republican Rome: 327-70 B.C.*, Oxford 1985 and M. Holleaux, Maurice, *Rome, la Grèce et les monarchies hellénistiques au IIIe siècle avant J.-C. (273-205)*, Paris 1935.

A – Hellenistic and Roman officers

The figure on the left wears a decorated tunic and high boots, or *calcei*. This were flat-soled, usually hobnailed boots, which covered the foot and ankle. Laces or crossed thongs were used to secure the boot. He is defended by an iron cuirass, vaguely similar to the corselet found at Vergina in the tomb attributed to Philip II. Shaped as a *linothorax*, with two rows of leather *pteryges* ending in a golden fringe, covering the upper arms, it is decorated with two *Victoriae*, and a central head of Medusa. The round shield, an *aspis*, is decorated with the head of Mars. He wears a mantle, or *chlamis*, quite similar to the Roman *paludametum*. His head is covered with an Attic-Boeothian helmet with cheekpieces. The crest is made with horse hair.

Also, the figure on the left wears a decorated tunic and high boots, or *calcei*. He is defended by a muscled cuirass. Both his cuirass as well as the Attic helmet with cheek pieces trace their source of inspiration to a statue, today in the castle of Rhodes, probably dated to the middle of the third century BCE. Under the bronze muscled cuirass, the figure wears a *subarmalis*, which ends in two rows of leather *pteryges* ending in a golden fringe, and also shorter *pteryges* covering the upper arms.

three years earlier. The text of this *senatus consultum* could be divided in four parts. The first part deals with the legal status of the commanding officers, the second part, the most important, focuses on the legal status of the common soldier, the third part is dedicated to the legal status of the equites, or the members of the equestrian class, and the last clause, throw an interesting light on the legal status of the *socii*, or the Italic continent.

Thus, it seems that the surviving consul Terentius Varo, as well as with the *tribuni militum*, the officers, were exonerated from any responsibility or mismanagement in the defeat. Thus, both the consul as well as the tribunes could continue their *cursus honorum* undisturbed. However, the common soldiers became the scapegoat of the defeat. The soldiers were accused of cowardice in front of the enemy. Thus, they were stripped of their civil rights, and sent to Sicily in exile till the end of the war or till any Carthaginian army was in Italy. Moreover, they were denied both the possibility to face the enemy in battle and the award of any military decoration. The pay of the soldiers was taken away only the first year (Livy, *History of Rome* XXIII, 31). From then, onwards, it seems that the *legiones cannenses* continued to receive their pay. Thus, the legal status of the *legiones cannenses* changed from that of citizen soldiers to that of mercenaries. They were paid, but they are not considered any more citizens. On the other hand, according to Livy, all the cavalrymen, or all the soldiers who stemmed from the equestrian class, were deprived of their state horses as punishment. Moreover, their military service was to be lengthened, and the years of service done with state given horses were not counted, but each cavalryman was obliged to serve ten more years with his own horse, purchased at his expenses.

Thus, the *equites* were not deprived of their citizenship, but their military service was lengthened. As previously stated, the last part of the *senatus consultum* deals with the fate of the Italic contingent. Probably, the common Italic soldiers shared in the fate of the legionaries. However, as with their Roman counterparts, the Italic horsemen were probably punished less harshly. Livy wrote clearly the source of the Italic contingent. They were Latins and allies from colonies of Ardea, Nepotes, Sutrii, Alba, Carseoli, Sora, Suessa, Circeii, Sezia, Cales, Narnia and Interama. However, the Italic contingent reacted differently from the Romans. In 209 BCE the Italic contingent mutinied, although according to the *senatus consultum*, their fate was no harsher than that of the Roman legions. The Senate reacted quickly and the mutinous Italic soldiers were sent home.

According to the Senate's judgment, so well-illustrated by Livy, these soldiers did not stand at the onslaught of Cannae and died as Romans, but fled away ignominiously from the fury of the enemy, and, thus, they had to be punished. Besides, because of their behavior they had lost the right to be considered full-fledged citizens of the Roman Republic. But this punishment was different from the one usually met by Roman legions in similar cases. This time, as they failed their fellow citizens, they had to be dramatically separated from the whole citizen's body and cast out from the civic society. And yet, on the other hand, the state gave to these soldiers a second chance to redeem themselves. Thus, this civic exile was reduced in terms of time and it was not definitive. But once more this chance was given to the soldiers, to the *legiones cannenses* as a collective body, not as individuals. Was really the Senate was convinced that the survivors of Cannae were cowards? Cowardice was not the real issue. It was clear to everyone that someone had to pay for the defeat, "pour encourager les autres". The culprits could not have been searched among the members of the senatorial class, nor the consul, nor the *tribuni militum*. Besides, the cavalrymen, coming from the equestrian class, could be penalized up to a certain point only. For example, they could not have been deprived of their citizenship. Their punishment was thus more symbolic than real. Thus, only the legionaries, the common soldier, coming from the lower classes and the Italic allies could be punished harshly.

3. PECULIAR COMMITMENT AND LOYALTY TO THE WARLORDS

The *Senatus consultum* created a force of mercenaries, skilled and professional soldiers, more devoted and faithful to their commanders than to the Roman Republic. In fact, these units probably served, one after the other, the first warlords of Rome, Marcellus, the conqueror of Syracuse, Scipio Africanus, who defeated Hannibal at Zama, and Flamininus, who defeated the legendary Macedonian phalanx. All these three warlords were imbued of Greek culture as well as of Hellenistic values, and molded themselves on the figure of Alexander the Great. Therefore, all these leaders were formed to the cult of the personality and on the image of absolute leadership, and thus, their politic prototype was quite different, if not in total opposition, to the traditional collectivistic values of the *patres conscripti* of the Roman Republic, such as Quintus Fabius Maximus and of course Cato the Elder. Thus, the soldiers of the *legiones cannenses* established a new informal relationship of trust with their commanders. Their *fides* was devolved from the Roman Republic, the state, to their own commanders, warlords imbued of Hellenistic values, alien to the spirit of Rome.

The first warlord that the *legiones cannenses* served was Marcus Claudius Marcellus, the future conqueror of the Greek city of Syracuse. The soldiers of the *legiones cannenses* met for the first time Marcellus immediately after Cannae, well before the *Senatus consultum* was passed, when they were put under his command with the purpose of assisting in the immediate defense of Rome. Thus, fighting under Marcellus's orders, they were successful in keeping Hannibal at bay. Slightly later, after the passing of the *Senatus consultum*, and once the immediate danger to Rome, the *urbs*, was passed, the *legiones cannenses*, were sent far away in exile to Sicily. Although the original purpose of their sojourn in the province of Sicily was to serve as garrison, the military developments, mainly the rebellion of Syracuse, brought the *legiones cannenses* once more under the orders of Marcellus. The legionaries distinguished themselves in the last stage of the war in Sicily, probably at the siege of Syracuse. Thus, although the Senate would have preferred to keep them away from the field of battle, the *patres conscripti* gave to Marcellus the possibility to use these units in the field. As they were the most professional and trained units at his disposition, and as these units already had served under his command, Marcellus did not hesitate to demonstrate sympathy forging a peculiar bond between the commander and his soldiers. He was right and the *legiones cannenses* behaved successfully.

However, the most important warlord associated to the *legiones cannenses* was Publius Cornelius Scipio Africanus. After the war in Sicily, the *legiones cannenses* passed once more a long period garrisoning Sicily, with their moral at the lowest ebb. But, then, Fortuna once again smiled to the veterans of Cannae, as the real occasion to excel came some years later under the orders of Scipio Africanus. As Marcellus, also Publius Cornelius Scipio, the future Africanus, had enjoyed a previous, a personal relationship with the *legiones cannenses*, when he was a young military tribune of one of the original Cannae legions. The relationship developed between Scipio and the *legiones cannenses* was quite peculiar, not just that of *patronus – cliens*, but also one that made evident the shared dangers and the real comradeship, which bonded the commander to his soldiers. As the *legiones cannenses* were outcasts and not Roman citizens, the bond between the warlord and its soldiers transcended the one the Roman commanders had with their citizen soldiers. This association between the warlord and his soldiers was quite similar to that current in the Hellenistic armies, established by Antigonus Monophtalmus.[3] Scipio reorganized tactically the Cannae's legions on new lines, which became the bulk of his volunteer army. The *legiones cannenses* fought successfully with Scipio in Africa and at Zama.

Once back in Italy, Scipio was successful in settling the Cannae's veterans in the most fertile

---

3   On Antigonus Monophtalmus see R.A. Billows, *Antigonus the One-Eyed and the Creation of the Hellenistic State, Hellenistic Culture and Society*, Berkeley 1997, mainly pp. 242-250.

lands of Italy. Scipio not only quashed the *senatus consultum* that had established the *legiones cannenses* more than fourteen years earlier, but he also had his own soldiers settled in the most fertile lands of Italy. According to Livy, Scipio received from the Senate for the African army land allotments in Apulia and Samnium (Livy, *History of Rome* XXXI, 4). These lands had been confiscated to the original Samnite and Apulian owners, as they had switched their allegiance from Rome to Hannibal.[4] According to Livy the *senatus consultum* gave to the *praetor urbanus* Marcus Junius the task to appoint a board of ten *decemviri* to survey and assign the lands of Samnium and Apulia. The ten *decemviri* were Publius Servilius, Quintus Caecilius Metellus, Gaius Servilius Geminus, Marcus Servilius Geminus, Lucius Hostilius Cato, Aulus Hostilius Cato, Publius Villius Tappulus, Marcus Fulvius Flaccus, Publius Aelius Paetus, Titus Quintius Flamininus. Some of the decemviri, appointed in 201 BCE to assign land to Scipio African's veterans, such as Publius Villius Tappulus and Titus Quintius Flamininus, were probably close collaborators. The allotment of lands to veterans was an old established custom in the Roman Republic. However, this time Scipio followed a new pattern, very different from the past. For the first time, it was the victorious general who settled his soldiers through his preponderant influence in the Senate and on the Roman political scene, and not the Senate as a body. Thus, the Senate was no more seen as the main actor in the allotment of lands, but only as a passive bystander, whose only task was to give his passive acquiescence. These lands were seen as the legitimate bounty that the victorious generals could distribute after his victory to his own faithful soldiers. Thus, the soldiers were grateful not to the Senate that revoked their citizenship and divorced them from their civic rights, but to the warlord who gave them back their civil rights and land parcels on which to start a new life. The Cannae's veterans were aware that they owned these lands to Scipio, and of course their best interest was to continue to serve their *patronus* as faithful *clientes*. This close relationship between the Scipio, the victorious commander, and his veterans, the *legiones cannenses*, reflected the settlement of veterans of Marius and Sulla, as well as the later settlements of Pompey and Julius Caesar, and of course the well-known veteran's settlement of Augustus in Italy on confiscated land after Philippi and Nau*lochos*.[5]

The last of the Roman warlords of the middle Republic closely associated with the *legiones cannenses* was Titus Quinctius Flamininus. The end of the Second Punic War was not the end of the

---

4   On Titus Quintius Flamininus see also Plutarch, *Flamininus* 1, 4 and 2, 1. See also H.H. Scullard, *Scipio Africanus, Soldier and Politician*, London 1970, pp. 181-182, p. 181 note 149.

5   See on the settlements of veterans in the Late Republic E. Gruen, *The Last Generation of the Roman Republic*, Berkeley 1995, mainly pp. 10, 37, 378, mainly pp. 387-404, 501. See also P. Southern, *Augustus*, London 1998, p. 66-67 on Philippi, p. 87 on Nau*lochos*. See also note on p. 226 with bibliography.

B –Centurio Primus Pilus and Tribunus Militum

The figure on the left, a *centurio* primus pilus wears a simple tunic and caligae, hobnailed sandals. His cuirass traces its source of inspiration in Etruscan figurines depicting the god Mars.

He wears a leather corselet covered with bronze plates, shaped as a linothorax, with a row of pteryges, which alternates a simple stripe of leather, and a stripe of leather covered by a bronze plate. He wears a mantle, or paludametum. His head is covered with an iron Attic helmet with cheekpieces and a crest of horse hair. Two full length greaves defend his lower legs up to the knees. The greaves, which by now, followed the anatomy of the leg, had rings for straps.

The figure on the right, a young tribunus *militum*, wears a decorated tunic and high boots, or calcei. His muscled cuirass as well as the Attic helmet with cheek pieces a crest of horse hair traces their source of inspiration to a statue, today in the castle of Rhodes, probably dated to the middle of the third century BCE. Under the cuirass, the figure wears a subarmalis, which ends in red leather pteryges, with two upper rows of larger shorter and larger pteryges reinforced with bronze discs, and a lower row made of longer pteryges. His sword is a Greek xyphos.

1

2

▲ Marble bust of Hannibal Barca in the Bardo National Museum.

legiones cannenses. It seems that the peace with Carthage did bring the dissolution of this now veteran body. Thus, the veterans received land allotments in southern Italy as reward for their services through the influence of their commander Scipio on the Roman Senate.

However, as it was clear that the *legiones cannenses* had now become the most successful unit of the whole Roman army, once Rome begun the Second Macedonian War, the *legiones cannenses* were once more mobilized. This time the veterans of Cannae were volunteers, and they became the bulk of the army of Sulpicius Galba and then of Flamininus. Under the orders of Flamininus the *legiones cannenses* defeated the Macedonian phalanx of Philip V at Cynoscephalae.

THE MANIPULAR LEGION

5 Turma of cavalry each arranged in 10 files and 3 ranks

5 Turma of cavalry each arranged in 10 files and 3 ranks

1200 Hastati (using Pila) - each century 20 files and 3 ranks

1200 Principes (using Pila) - each century 20 files and 3 ranks

600 Triarii (using Hastae) in 10 files and 6 ranks

Velites (after withdrawal from skirmishing)

▲ The Organization of the *manipular* legion

▲ *Silver denarius, minted in 112-111 BCE, depicting on the obverse the head of Mars, or possibly Scipio Africanus the Elder, wearing crested Corinthian helmet, looking right; monogram with the inscription CN BLASIO CN F, with behind it a prow. On the reverse is depicted the Capitoline Triad, Jupiter, holding scepter and thunderbolt, standing facing Juno and Minerva. The inscription on the reverse reads Roma, Π in field.*

4. THE EVOLUTION AND CHANGING OF THE TACTICAL COMPOSITION OF THE LEGIONS

The dramatic *Senatus consultum* of 215 BCE influenced the development of the tactical composition of the *legiones cannenses*. At their beginning the *legiones cannenses* presented a tactical composition, an armament and equipment identical to that of all the other legions (the *Manipula*r Legion). Yet, with time the *legiones cannenses* changed in their strength, composition and in its tactic division. Thus, the *legiones cannenses* that faced Hannibal at Zama were much more similar in their strength, composition, and tactical division to the legions of the Late Republic and of the early Empire than to those described by Polybius. However, it is difficult to understand if this metamorphosis followed the empirical needs of the moment or it was brought up by theoretical requirements. All the legions, which would take part at the battle of Cannae, were organized in an identical way to the other legions levied during the Second Punic War, the *manipula*r legion. According to Livy, the typical legion of the Second Punic War includes 4000 infantrymen and 300 cavalrymen. According to Polybius, however, a Roman legion numbered generally 4200 infantrymen and 300 cavalrymen (Livy, *History of Rome* XXI, 17 and Polybius, *Histories* VI, 20). The infantry was divided in light troops and heavy infantry. The light troops or *velites* fought as skirmishers. In a legion there were 1200 *velites* and 3000 heavy infantry. Of these the youngest 1200, or *hastati*, formed the first line, those older, the *principes*, formed the second line, and the veterans or *triarii*, 600 in a legion, formed the third line. The main tactic subdivision of the Roman legion in this period was the *manipulum*. A legion was divided in 30 *manipula*. Each *manipulum* was composed of 120 men heavy armed (*hastati* and *principes*), and circa 50-60 light armed *velites*, that bring the total strength of a *manipulum* to 180 men. However, a *manipulum* of *triarii* is composed of 60 men and 40 *velites*. The 300 cavalrymen were divided in 10 *turmae*, each composed of 30 men, divided in 3 *decuriae*, commanded by a *decurio*, seconded by an *optio*.

The *socii*, or allies' contingents had a similar organization to that of the Roman legion. Thus, each contingent consisted in 4200 infantrymen divided in 30 *manipula*. However, Polybius emphasizes that the allies had 900 cavalrymen divided in 30 *turmae*, or thrice the number of cavalrymen in a Roman legion. The hierarchy of command of the *manipula*r legion began with the consul, who commanded two legions and the correspondent allied contingent. The legion itself was commanded by six *tribuni militum*, who were, irrespective of their age, the senior officers. The tribuni selected the junior officer. Thus, for each *manipulum*, an officer, the *centurio prior*, was selected. This officer in turn chose as subordinate another officer, the *centurio posterior*. The only *centurion* who was considered as senior officer was the first *centurion* of the first *manipulum* of the *triarii*, or primus pilus, who sat

---

C – Centurio

The figure wears a decorated tunic and high boots, or *perones* in use among common people. Contrary to the *calcei*, the perones were closed. He is defended by a *lorica hamata* and on his head, he wears a Montefortino helmet. Around 300 BCE mail was invented, probably by the Celts. This type of *lorica hamata* was cut like a Greek linen cuirass. It was long enough to reach the hips. A similar example is the statue of the Celtic warrior from Vachères. The remains of a mail cuirass from Ciumestyi shows that *lorica hamata* was made of alternate rows of punched and butted rings. Also riveted rings could be used. These rings are 7 mm in diameter. The Greek style mail cuirass had a fastener which was fixed to the shirt and hooked on to the two shoulder pieces. He wears leather *pterygges* under the *lorica hamata*. The *lorica hamata* is depicted on the reliefs of the monument of Aemilius Paullus at Delphi, on the altar of Domitius Ahenobarbus, and on reliefs from the Temple of Athena, at Pergamum. Also, the Montefortino helmet originated among the Celts around 300 BCE. First adopted by the Etruscans, later on, the Romans used it till the late first century BCE, and even onwards. These helmets are distinguished by a conical or round shape with a raised up central knob, a projecting neck guard, and cheek pieces. While in this case, the cheek pieces were made in bronze, often poorer soldiers had to content of cheek pieces made in leather or perishable material. His Montefortino is crowned by a central crest of horse hair and three feathers, a decorative feature taken from the Saminites. In his hand he holds a vine stick. The *vitis*, mentioned by Tacitus, indicated his task.

in council with the tribuni. *Centurions* also appointed for each maniple two rearguard officers or *optio*. Other officers were the signifer, or standard bearer, cornicen, or musician, and the tesserarius, who distributed the daily corvées.[6] It seems that till Scipio reorganized these legions, following new tactical lines, they kept the *manipulum* as their main basic tactical unit. Scipio's tactical reorganization, which probably was empirical and had already began in Spain, focused on three main aspects, a new numeration of the surviving units, a tactic inner reorganization of the units, which emphasized the importance of the *cohors*, and the detachment of the *velites* from the *manipulum*.

First of all, the *legiones cannenses* received a number, and now these appear as the 5th and 6th legions. The purpose of this was to emphasize that the two legions were no more a penal unit, but units similar to all the other legions composed of citizen soldier citizens.

Scipio also increased the numbers of soldiers in each legion from 4200 to a total of 6200 infantrymen and 300 cavalrymen.[7] According to Livy, Scipio achieved this purpose adding new soldiers that he brought from Italy. Scipio, thus, created a unit much more similar to the Late Republican and Early Imperial counterparts, which numbered 5500 men.

Moreover, the *manipula* of *principes*, *hastati*, and *triarii* were grouped together in a *cohors*, which lacks the *velites*. Thus, Livy, in his account of the battle of Zama, narrates that the *cohortes* were the main division of the army. Besides, Livy narrates that as soon as Scipio arrived to Sicily, he divided the volunteers in *centuriae* (Livy, *History of Rome* XXIX, 1). Only one hundred year later, in the wake of Marius's reforms, the *centuria* would become the main tactic subdivision of the legion, taking the place of the *manipulum*. One of the consequences of this reorganization was that the *velites* were detached "en bloc" from the *manipulum* and they were grouped together in a different formation.

How Scipio's *legiones cannenses* looked like? There are two different *options* to better understand the innovative character of the tactical reforms introduced by Scipio.

The first possibility is that the legion conserved the traditional organization of the *cohors*, composed of two *manipula* of *hastati* and *principes* each numbering 120 men, and a *manipulum* of *triarii* numbering 60 men. Each *centuria* numbered between 30 *triarii* and 60 *hastati* and *principes*. In this case the legion was divided in twenty *cohortes*. Therefore, in this framework, the *centuria* did not play any important part. The second possibility is that the later *centuriae*, numbering 80 men, became the basic tactical unit of the legion. Thus, each legion was divided in thirteen *cohortes*. Each *cohors* was divided in three *manipula* of 160 men. Each *manipulum* was divided in two *centuriae* of 80 men. In this case the *triarii* units numbered the same as those composed by *hastati* and *principes*. This second reconstruction, definitely more similar to that of the Late Republic and early Imperial legions, seems to be more probable, because the importance of the *centuria* as the basic tactical unit is more emphasized.[8] This also explains the passage of Livy referring to the *centuriae* previously quoted, otherwise difficult to explain. In fact, the *centuria* as basic subdivision of the legion existed in name but not in fact inside the *manipular* legion. Thus, a legion was composed by 60 *centuriae*, each numbering 60 men. Two *centuriae* thus formed a *manipulum*. However, during the Second Punic War, the Roman army fought as *manipula*, not as *centuriae*. Indeed, the creation of this new tactical unit of heavy armed infantry (*principes*, *hastati*, and *triarii*) which privileged the use of the cohorts is confirmed by the description of the tactic used by Scipio at the battle of Zama by Polybius (Polybius, *Histories* XV, 9) as well as Livy (Livy, *History of Rome* XXX, 33).[9]

6   See P. Connolly, *Greece and Rome at War*, London 1981, pp. 129-134.

7   This is not accepted by Lazenby. See A.F. Lazenby, *Hannibal's War, A Military History of the Second Punic War*, Warminster 1978, p. 202.

8   See P. Connolly, *Greece and Rome at War*, London 1981, pp. 216-217.

9   Livy narrates that the *cohortes* were the main division of the army. Moreover, Polybius as well as Livy emphasize that Scipio, while drawing up his army in their normal three lines, however he gave order that the *manipula* were to be drawn up one behind the other leaving gaps through the legions. See also P. Connolly, *Greece and Rome at War*, London 1981, p. 204. On the organization of Scipio's army see G. Brizzi, *Scipione ed Annibale. La guerra per salvare Roma*, Bari 2007, pp. 166-168.

5. THE HISTORY OF THE LEGIONES CANNENSES

A. THE LEGIONS LEVIED IN 218 BCE

The *legiones cannenses* created by a *senatus consultum*, stemmed in the eight legions that took part in the battle of Cannae. The first two of these legions were levied in 218 BCE, at the beginning of the Second Punic War (1st and 2nd legions) under the command of the consul Publius Cornelius Scipio. How many legions were formed in 218 BCE, four or six legions? Polybius and Livy diverge on the total strength of the army. According to Polybius only four legions were levied (Polybius, *Histories* III, 40). However, Livy emphasizes that a total of six legions were levied (Livy, *History of Rome* XXI, 6, 17). According to most scholars the data of Livy this time is more valuable than that of Polybius. Thus, according to De Sanctis and Toynbee and Goldsworthy six legions were levied in the year 218 BCE. According to De Sanctis four legions were sent to Gallia Cisalpina (1st, 2nd, 3rd, 4th), and two to Spain with Scipio's brother (5th and 6th). [10]

It seems that the first two legions (1st and 2nd) once levied were given to the consul Publius Cornelius Scipio the Elder, together with other two (5th and 6th). These last two legions remained in Spain with the Scipiones till were wiped out in 210 BCE. Tiberius Sempronius Longus received the other two legions (3rd and 4th). The purpose of Tiberius Sempronius Longus was the invasion of Africa, while that of Publius Cornelius Scipio the Elder's was to reach Spain, his *provincia*, or the area where he exercised his *imperium* or command, and join battle with the Carthaginian army. It was not to be. An insurrection of Celtic tribesmen, the Boii, in Northern Italy followed by another tribe, the Insubres changed dramatically the situation. Thus, according to Polybius, the two legions of Publius Cornelius Scipio (1st and 2nd) were given in command to the *praetor* C. Atilius and were sent to Gallia Cisalpina in support of a third legion, levied the preceding year (Polybius 4th). Meanwhile Scipio resumed his original purpose. Moreover, Scipio the Elder under his orders the Italic contingent levied for the occasion (Polybius, *Histories* III, 40). Livy, however, offers a different narration (Livy, *History of Rome* XXI, 26). Scipio the Elder sent to Atilius in Cisalpine Gaul only one legion (the 2nd?), then, he levied one more legion and marched to Spain with the allied contingent and three more legions (1st, 5th and 6th). Scipio's military operations in southern France resulted in a failure, as he did not catch up with Hannibal's army. [11] Besides, the situation faced by the *praetor* C. Atilius in Cisalpine Gaul was dramatic. Scipio has no alternative but to hurry back to Northern Italy with one legion (1st?) and face there the Carthaginians. Hannibal had by then crossed the Alps. [12] Thus, Publius Cornelius Scipio the Elder left his two other legions (5th and 6th) and the Italic contingent to his brother Gnaeus to carry on the war in Spain. Scipio the Elder, then, took back the command of his 2nd legion from the *praetors* Manlius and Atilius in the plain of the Po (Polybius, *Histories* III, 56, Livy, *History of Rome* XXI, 39). Scipio then moved his army to Placentia and then pitched his camp in front of the river Ticinum, where he is faced by Hannibal. A cavalry skirmish at Ticino was concluded with the Romans flight.

The battle of Ticinum is very important as for the first time the young Publius Cornelius Scipio, son of the consul Publius Cornelius Scipio, is associated to one of the future *legiones cannenses*. Livy, while relating the skirmish on Ticinum, narrates that the young Publius Cornelius Scipio saved the life of his father, the consul Publius Cornelius Scipio (Livy, *History of Rome* XXI, 46). Thus, the young Publius Cornelius Scipio, that one day will lead the at Zama, served already in 218 BCE as military tribune in one of the two legions levied by his father. It seems that the young Publius Cornelius Scipio

---

10   See A. Goldsworthy, *The Fall of Carthage, The Punic Wars 265-146 BC*, London 2003, pp. 150-151 on the allocation of the legions to the two consuls. See also A.J. Toynbee, *Hannibal's Legacy, The Hannibal War's effects on Roman Life, Rome and her Neighbours after Hannibal's exit*, London 1965, pp. 648-649.

11   See A. Goldsworthy, *The Fall of Carthage, The Punic Wars 265-146 BC*, London 2003, pp. 151-163.

12   On Hannibal military thinking, best read G. Brizzi, *Annibale, come un autobiografia*, Le vite, Milano 1994.

▲ Bronze bust of Scipio Africanus the Elder, mid-first century BCE (Villa of the Papyri at Herculaneum; National Archaeological Museum, Naples, Inv. No. 5634).

continued to serve in the legion till the battle of Cannae, to which he took part, still in the capacity of military tribune (Livy, *History of Rome* XXII, 53).[13] This episode could corroborate the fact that the 1st and 2nd legions served at the battle of Cannae.

Afterwards Scipio the Elder retired to Placentia, and subsequently pitched camp near the Trebia with his army (1st and 2nd Legions). There, the other consul, Tiberius Sempronius Longus and his army joined force with Scipio (3rd and 4th Legions). The battle of Trebia which followed also ended in a defeat for the Romans. According to Livy (Livy, *History of Rome* XXI, 55), the whole army of the two consuls totaled between 16.000 and 18.000 (the 1st, 2nd, 3rd, 4th legions) and included also the Italic contingent and the Cenoman Gauls. Polybius writes that Tiberius Sempronius Longus faced Hannibal with 16.000 legionary infantry (Polybius, *Histories* III, 72). The Romans total losses were around 15.000 men (Polybius, *Histories* III, 70-74 and Livy, *History of Rome* XXI, 53-56).[14]

Scipio the Elder, however, was successful in reorganizing his army well after the defeat. In fact, he moved his legions (1st and 2nd Legions) in winter quarters to Placentia, while and the remaining of Longus's army (3rd and 4th Legions) moved to Cremona (Livy, *History of Rome* XXI, 56). The morale of Scipio the Elder's soldiers was still high. Thus, in a skirmish near Placentia as Hannibal tried to conquer a food deposit during the night, Scipio's soldiers defeated the Carthaginians (Livy, *History of Rome* XXI, 57). Scipio the Elder's soldiers were still battle worthy and their morale did not suffer much after the defeat of Trebia. Scipio the Elder's army then moved from Placentia to Etruria, while the remains of Longus army moved from Cremona to Rimini. Thus, till Cannae, the only military experience of the 1st and 2nd legions were pitched battles with the Gauls in northern Italy that obviously involved both infantry and cavalry, as well as the cavalry skirmish at Ticino, which was concluded with a defeat, and probably a minor role in the battle of Trebia.

B.   THE LEGIONS LEVIED IN 217 BCE

At least two other legions, the 12th and the 13th, which would later take part at the battle of Cannae, were levied by the consul Gnaus Servilius Geminus at the beginning of the consular year in March 217 BCE (Polybius, *Histories* III, 75). These two legions were inactive till after the battle of Lake Trasimenus, with the exception of some skirmishes and the siege of a Gaulish *oppidum* (Livy, *History of Rome* XXII, 9). These legions were stationed at Ariminum and in Etruria, where the consul hoped to oppose any enemy advance from that quarter (Polybius, *Histories* III, 75, 77). However, according to Connolly, not two, but four new legions were levied at the beginning of 217 BCE. While Gaius Quintus Flaminius levied the 10th and the 11th legions, Gnaeus Servilius Geminus levied the 12th and 13th legions, already mentioned. Noticeably the Romans wished to fill the void caused by the Gauls and the first year of campaigning.

Moreover, a second group of legions, the 14th, 15th, 16th, and 17th was levied later in the year 217 BCE after the Trasimene defeat by the *dictator* Fabius Maximus and the *magister equitum* Minucius Rufus (Polybius, *Histories* III, 88. Livy, *History of Rome* XXII, 11).[15]

---

13   On the earlier years of Scipio Africanus, see G. Brizzi, *Scipione ed Annibale. La guerra per salvare Roma*, Bari 2007, pp. 17-32. See A. Goldsworthy, *The Fall of Carthage, The Punic Wars 265-146 BC*, London 2003, pp. 169-173 on the skirmish of Ticino.
14   On the battle of Trebia see A. Goldsworthy, *The Fall of Carthage, The Punic Wars 265-146 BC*, London 2003, pp. 173-181.
15   However, according to De Sanctis, the legions under the command of Geminus were the 10th and 11th. Besides, later on, only two legions were levied by the *cunctator*, the 12th and the 13th. See A.J. Toynbee, *Hannibal's Legacy, The Hannibal War's effects on Roman Life, Rome and her Neighbours after Hannibal's exit*, London 1965, pp. 648-649. According to Connolly the second group of legions levied in 217 BCE were the 14th, 15th, 16th, and 17th. See P. Connolly, *Greece and Rome at War*, London 1981, p. 178.

Besides, according to Connolly and other scholars such as De Sanctis and Toynbee at least three other legions were levied, the 7th and 8th legions, that were sent to Sicily, and the 9th that was sent to Sardinia. Livy (Livy, *History of Rome* XXI, 63) states that Flaminius commanded the remains of the two legions of Sempronius Longus (3rd, 4th), as well as two more legions, previously under the command of the *praetor* C. Atilius (1st and 2nd). Yet, it seems puzzling that Flaminius faced Hannibal at Trasimene with four legions, all under strength.

In the wake of the disaster suffered on the Trasimene, the Roman senate appointed Quintus Fabius Maximus *dictator* for the remaining of the year. The newly elected *dictator* strived to avoid pitched battles against Hannibal. Thus, till the battle of Cannae, the new legions got an impressive amount of marches, countermarches, and of course some skirmishes, but the tactic of Quintus Fabius Maximus, the *cunctator*, forbade any pitched battle.[16] The *cunctator* divided part of his army in two (Livy, *History of Rome* XXII, 27-28), a half under his command (14th and 15th), and half under Minucius's command (16th and 17th). Besides, according to Connolly, Servilius Geminus brought with him to Narnia, together with the 12th and the 13th legions, also the 1st and 2nd legions. As well stated by Connolly, the common characteristic of these legions, which would later take part in the battle of Cannae, the 1st, 2nd, 12th, and 13th, was their lacking of cavalry. In fact, the cavalry of the 1st and 2nd legions had been exterminated at Ticinum, and the cavalry of the 12th and 13th legions, commanded by Centenius, had been destroyed by Maharbal after the Trasimenus. Thus, it is possible that in most of the military operations these four legions played a secondary role.[17]

The four new legions, levied by the *dictator*, could get experience, albeit in skirmishes, while the other four legions, or only two of them, which lacked cavalry, were used in supportive role. Quintus Fabius Maximus faced the Carthaginians near Aecae (Polybius, *Histories* III, 88). Hannibal endeavored to unnerve the Romans by attacking, but the *dictator* ordered the soldiers not to leave the camp and accept a pitched battle. Polybius also adds that to better succeed and probably to persuade Hannibal that a pitched battle was not worthwhile but dangerous, the *cunctator* always concentrated all his army together (Polybius, *Histories* III, 90). In the next six months, Fabius movements paralleled those of the enemy. Polybius is right when he states that "Fabius two purposes were to reduce enemy limited manpower and rebuild the spirit of his troops" (Polybius, *Histories* III, 90). According to Polybius, the *cunctator* suffered a decisive inferiority in cavalry, which prevented him from facing Hannibal in a pitched battle (Polybius, *Histories* III, 92). The main theatres of operations in the second half of 217 BCE, were first Campania and then Apulia. In Campania the main military operations covered the area from Beneventum (North) to the Volturno river (South) and the city of Venusia (East). In Apulia, the main theatre of operations was in the area between Gerunium, Larinum and Luceria. This time, however, most of the military operations were under the leadership of the impetuous Marcus Minucius. In fact, the *dictator* was for a while called back to Rome. The master equitum defeated in a small skirmish the Carthaginians. Elated by the success, Minucius strived to force the *dictator* to pitch battle with Hannibal. As Fabius Maximus let his *magister equitum* to follow his instinct, Minucius was defeated in a skirmish, and the *dictator* has to disengage him (Polybius, *Histories* III, 94, 100-104, 107 and Livy, *History of Rome* XXII, 18, 27-30).[18]

---

16   See A. Goldsworthy, *The Fall of Carthage, The Punic Wars 265-146 BC*, London 2003, pp. 190-192.
17   See P. Connolly, *Greece and Rome at War*, London 1981, p. 178.
18   See A. Goldsworthy, *The Fall of Carthage, The Punic Wars 265-146 BC*, London 2003, pp. 192-196.

C. 216 BCE: THE LEGIONS AT CANNAE

At the beginning of the year 216 BCE Lucius Aemilius Paulus and Gaius Terentius Varro were elected consuls. The Romans prepared for pitched battle. They did not wish to take any chance and fielded eight legions. According to Goldworthy the legions that were present at Cannae were the four legions commanded by Fabius Maximus, the 14th, 15th, 16th, and 17th and the four new legions levied by the two consuls at the beginning of the year 216 BCE, the 18th, 19th, 20th, and 21th.[19]

Another possibility is that the legions who took part in the battle consisted in the eight legions that were involved in the warfare against the Carthaginians (1st, 2nd, 12th, 13th, 14th, 15th, 16th, 17th). All these legions possessed a remarkable battle experience and could be considered veterans. The consul Lucius Aemilius Paulus took care that new levies filled the vacuum in the existing legions. Besides, he levied four new legions, the 18th, 19th, 20th and 21st. These new units did not take part in the battle, as they were not seasoned enough.

The composition of the legions that took part in the battle of Cannae is puzzling. While part of the soldiers were veterans of the battles fought in the previous years, at least half were inexperienced soldiers, just raw recruits. According to Polybius and Livy (Polybius, *Histories* III, 107 and Livy, *History of Rome* XXII, 36) the two consuls decided to bring the number of men for each legion from 4000 infantrymen and 200 horsemen to 5000 infantrymen and 300 cavalrymen. Thus, each of the eight legions received at least 1000 inexperienced infantryman, and the 1st, 2nd, 12th, and 13th legions received new and inexperienced cavalrymen, as these legions totally lacked the cavalry. Therefore,

19   See A. Goldsworthy, *The Fall of Carthage, The Punic Wars 265-146 BC*, London 2003, pp. 198-200

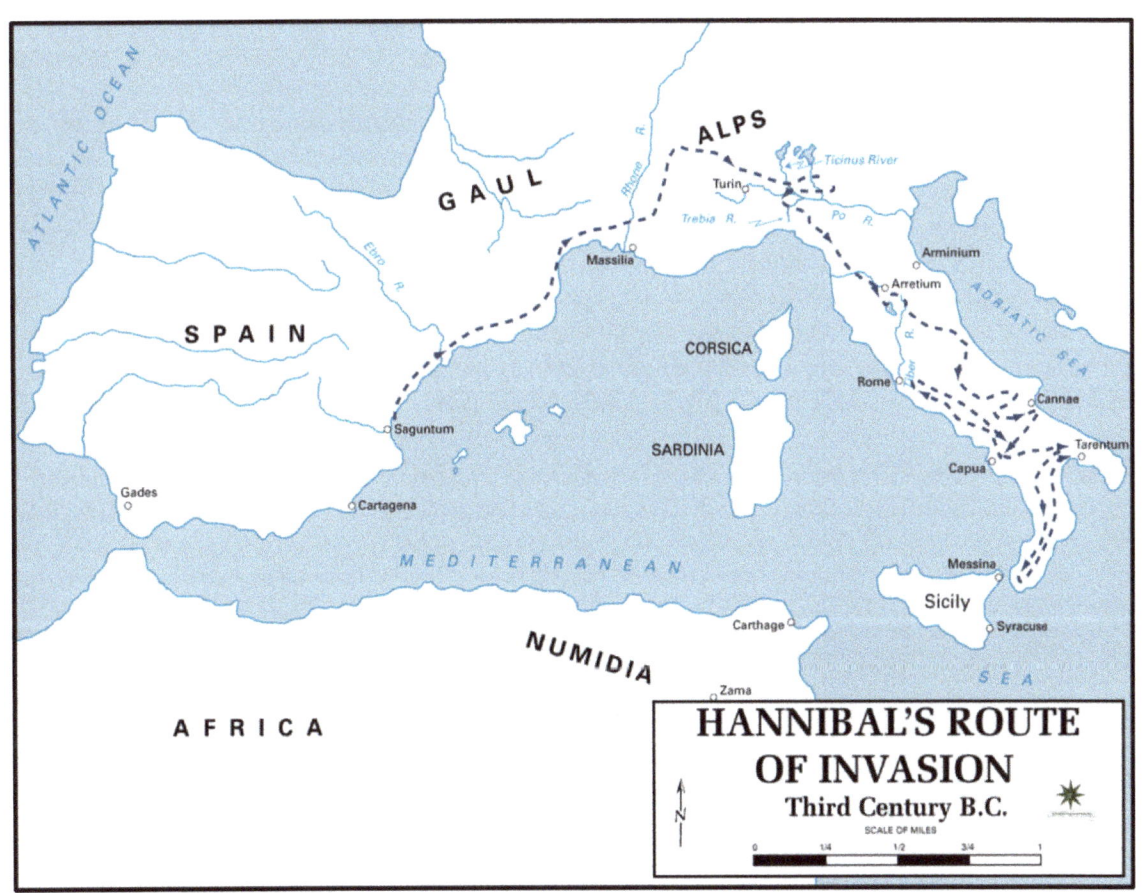

▲ Hannibal route of invasion

a fifth of the soldiers were completely inexperienced. Although the eight legions that were to face Hannibal at Cannae looked impressive, in reality were quite an unhappy, divided, and disorganized lot. The new reinforcements probably had no time to integrate between the veterans.[20]

The Roman legions were seconded by the faithful Italic *socii*. Livy writes that the Italic contingent that fought at Cannae were the Latins allies and Roman and Latin – Roman mixed colonists that came from Ardea, Nepotes, Sutrii, Alba, Carseoli, Sora, Suessa, Circeii, Sezia, Cales, Narnia and Interama (Livy, *History of Rome* XXVII, 9). Thus, the Romans brought with them the most faithful allies, Latins and Roman colonists. However, we do not know if the Italic allies had had any previous battle experience. Let's leave the description of the battle to our most valued sources, first Polybius, and then Livy.

"III.113 1 Next day it was Terentius' turn to take the command, and just after sunrise he began to move his forces out of both camps. Crossing the river with those from the larger camp he at once put them in order of battle, drawing up those from the other camp next to them in the same line, the whole army facing south. He stationed the Roman cavalry close to the river on the right wing and the foot next to them in the same line, placing the maniples closer together than was formerly the usage and making the depth of each many times exceed its front. The allied horse he drew up on his left wing, and in front of the whole force at some distance he placed his light-armed troops. The whole army, including the allies, numbered about eighty thousand foot and rather more than six thousand horse. Hannibal at the same time sent his slingers and pikemen over the river and stationed them in front, and leading the rest of his forces out of camp he crossed the stream in two places and drew them up opposite the enemy. On his left close to the river he placed his Spanish and Celtic horse facing the Roman cavalry, next these half his heavy-armed Africans, then the Spanish and Celtic infantry, and after them the other half of the Africans, and finally, on his right wing, his Numidian horse. After thus drawing up his whole army in a straight line, he took the central companies of the Spaniards and Celts and advanced with them, keeping rest of them in contact with these companies, but gradually falling off, so as to produce a crescent-shaped formation, the line of the flanking companies growing thinner as it was prolonged, his object being to employ the Africans as a reserve force and to begin the action with the Spaniards and Celts. 114 1 The Africans were armed in the Roman fashion, Hannibal having equipped them with the choicest of the arms captured in the previous battles. The shields of the Spaniards and Celts were very similar, but they swords were entirely different, those of the Spaniards thrusting with as deadly effect as they cut, but the Gaulish sword being only able to slash and requiring a long sweep to do so. As they were drawn up in alternate companies, the Gauls naked and the Spaniards in short tunics bordered with purple, their national dress, they p283 presented a strange and impressive appearance. The Carthaginian cavalry numbered about ten thousand, and their infantry, including the Celts, did not much exceed forty thousand. The Roman right wing was under the command of Aemilius, the left under that of Terentius, and the centre under the Consuls of the previous year, Marcus Atilius and Gnaeus Servilius. Hasdrubal commanded the Carthaginian left, Hanno the right, and Hannibal himself with his brother Mago the centre. Since the Roman army, as I said, faced

---

20   See P. Connolly, *Greece and Rome at War*, London 1981, p. 183 and A. Goldsworthy, *The Fall of Carthage, The Punic Wars 265-146 BC*, London 2003, p. 198 on the Roman legions' effectives at Cannae.

D - Veles

This figure wears a red tunic and *caligae*, hobnailed sandals. His head is protected by a simple Montefortino in bronze, lacking check pieces. However, his helmet is covered by a wolf head skin, which, according to Polybius, were given to those soldiers "who in the skirmishing or in similar circumstances in which there is no need to engage in single combat, have voluntarily and by choice placed themselves in danger." He is defended by a flat round shield in wood, the *parma*, relatively light. He carries the light form of *pilum*, and, probably a thrusting sword.

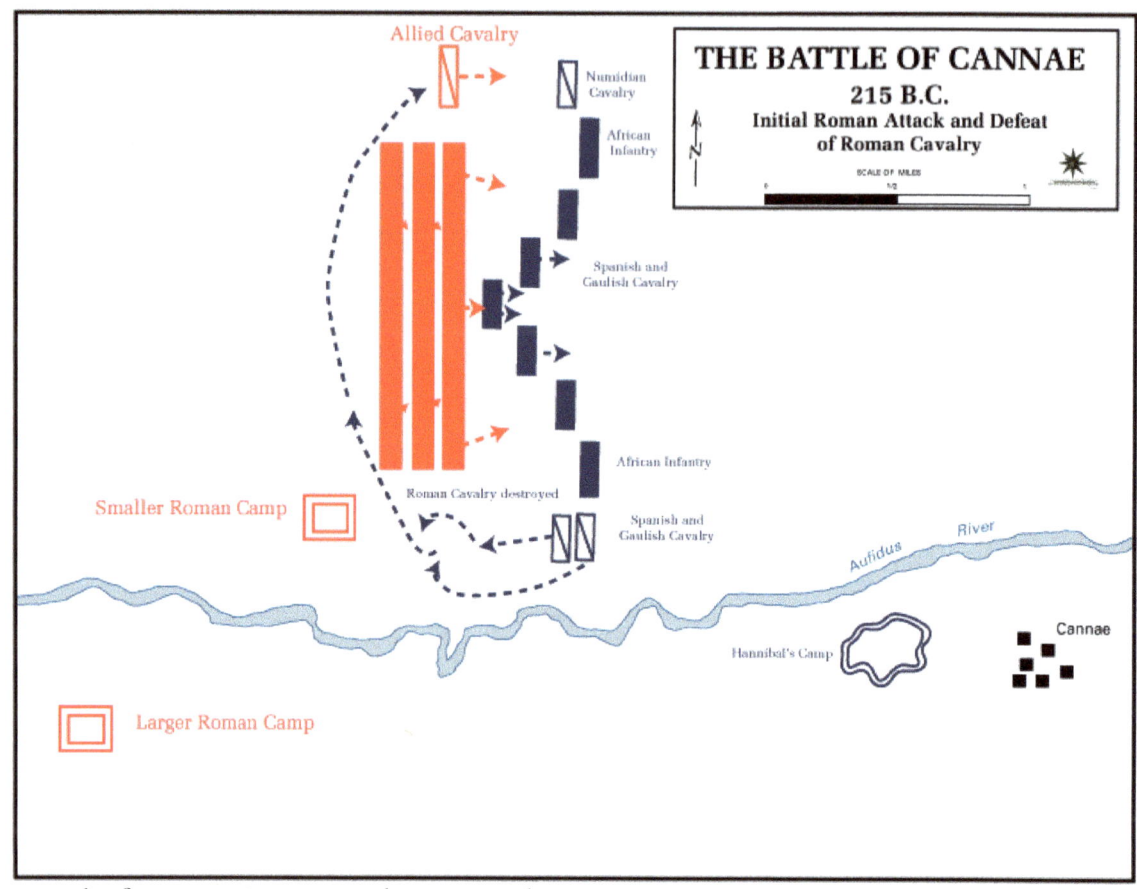

THE BATTLE OF CANNAE
215 B.C.
Initial Roman Attack and Defeat
of Roman Cavalry

SCALE OF MILES

▲ Battle of Cannae, 216 BCE – Initial Roman attack

south and the Carthaginians north, they were neither of them inconvenienced by the rising sun. 115 1 the advanced guards were the first to come into action, and at first when only the light infantry were engaged neither side had the advantage; but when the Spanish and Celtic horse on the left wing came into collision with the Roman cavalry, the struggle that ensued was truly barbaric; for there were none of the normal wheeling evolutions, but having once met they dismounted and fought man to man. The Carthaginians finally got the upper hand, killed most of the enemy in the mellay, all the Romans fighting with desperate bravery, and began to drive the rest along the river, cutting them down mercilessly, and it was now that the heavy infantry on each side took the place of the light-armed troops and met. For a time the Spaniards and Celts kept their ranks and struggled bravely with the Romans, but soon, borne down by the weight of the legions, they gave way and fell back, breaking up the crescent. The Roman maniples, pursuing them furiously, easily penetrated the enemy's front, since the Celts were deployed in a thin line while they themselves had crowded up from the wings to the centre where the fighting was going on. For the centres and wings did not come into action simultaneously, but the centres first, as the Celts were drawn up in a crescent and a long way in advance of their wings, the convex face of the crescent being turned towards the enemy. The Romans, however, following up the Celts and pressing on to the centre and that part of the enemy's line which was giving way, progressed so far that they now had the heavy-armed Africans on both of their flanks. Hereupon the Africans on the right wing facing to the left and then beginning from the right charged upon the enemy's flank, while those on the left faced to the right and dressing by the left, did the same, the situation itself indicating to them how to act. The consequence was that, as Hannibal had designed, the Romans, straying too far in pursuit of the Celts, were caught between the two divisions of the enemy, and they now

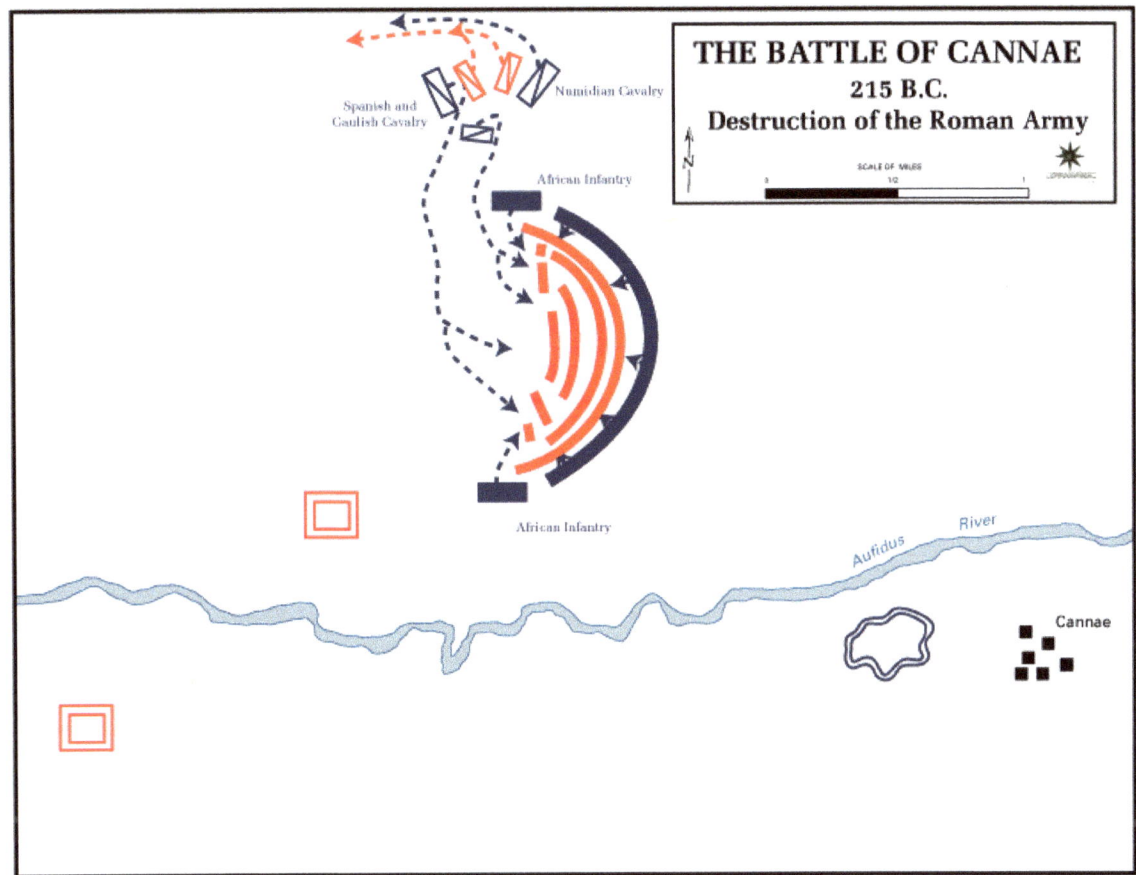

THE BATTLE OF CANNAE
215 B.C.
Destruction of the Roman Army

SCALE OF MILES

Numidian Cavalry

Spanish and
Gaulish Cavalry

African Infantry

African Infantry

Aufidus River

Cannae

▲ Battle of Cannae, 216 BCE – Annihilation of the Roman army

no longer kept their compact formation but turned singly or in companies to deal with the enemy who was falling on their flanks. 116 1 Aemilius, though he had been on the right wing from the outset and had taken part in the cavalry action, was still safe and sound; but wishing to act up to what he had said in his address to the troops, and to be present himself at the fighting, and seeing that the decision of the battle lay mainly with the legions, he rode along to the centre of the whole line, where he not only threw himself personally into the combat and exchanged blows with the enemy but kept cheering on and exhorting his men. Hannibal, who had been in this part of the field since the commencement of the battle, did likewise. 5 The Numidians meanwhile on the right wing, attacking the cavalry opposite them on the Roman left, neither gained any great advantage nor suffered any serious loss owing to their peculiar mode of fighting, but they kept the enemy's cavalry out of action by drawing them off and attacking them from all sides at once. Hasdrubal, having by this time cut up very nearly all the enemy's cavalry by the river, came up from the left to help the Numidians, and now the Roman allied horse, seeing that they were going to be charged by him, broke and fled. Hasdrubal at this juncture appears to have acted with great skill and prudence; for in view of the fact that the Numidians were very numerous and most efficient and formidable when in pursuit of a flying foe he left them to deal with the Roman cavalry and led his squadrons on to where the infantry were engaged with the object of supporting the Africans. Attacking the Roman legions in the rear and delivering repeated charges at various points all at once, he raised the spirits of the Africans and cowed and dismayed the Romans. It was here that Lucius Aemilius fell in the thick of the fight after receiving several dreadful wounds, and of him we may say that if there ever was a man who did his duty by his country both all through his life and in these last times, it was he. The Romans as long as they could turn and present a front on every side to the enemy, held out, but as the outer ranks continued to fall, and the rest were gradually huddled in and surrounded, they finally all were killed where they stood, among them Marcus and Gnaeus, the Consuls of the preceding year, who had borne themselves in the battle like brave men worthy of Rome. While this murderous combat was going on, the Numidians following up the flying cavalry killed most of them and unseated others. A few escaped to Venusia, among them being the Consul Gaius Terentius, who disgraced himself by his flight and in his tenure of office had been most unprofitable to his country. 117 1 Such was the outcome of the battle at Cannae between the Romans and Carthaginians, a battle in which both the victors and the vanquished displayed conspicuous bravery, as was evinced by the facts. For of the six thousand cavalry, seventy escaped to Venusia with Terentius, and about three hundred of the allied horse reached different cities in scattered groups. Of the infantry about ten thousand were captured fighting but not in the actual battle, while only perhaps three thousand escaped from the field to neighbouring towns. All the rest, numbering about seventy thousand, died bravely. Both on this occasion and on former ones their numerous cavalry had contributed most to the victory of the Carthaginians, and it demonstrated to posterity that in times of war it is better to give battle with half as many infantry as the enemy and an overwhelming force of cavalry than to be in all respects his equal. Of Hannibal's army there fell about four thousand Celts, fifteen hundred Spaniards and Africans and two hundred cavalry. 7 The Romans who were made prisoners were not in the battle for the following reason. Lucius had left a force of ten thousand foot in his own camp, in order that, if Hannibal, neglecting his camp, employed his whole army in the field, they might during the battle gain entrance there and capture all the enemy's baggage: if, on the other hand, Hannibal, guessing this danger, left a strong garrison in the camp, the force opposed to the Romans would be reduced in numbers. The circumstances of their capture were more or less as follows. Hannibal had left an adequate force to guard his camp, and when the battle opened, the Romans, as they had been ordered, delivered an assault on this force. At first they held out, but as they were beginning to be hard pressed, Hannibal, who was now victorious in every part of the field, came to their assistance, and routing the Romans shut them up in their camp. He killed two thousand of them and afterwards made all the rest prisoners. The Numidians also reduced the various strongholds throughout the country which had given shelter to the flying enemy and brought in the fugitives, consisting of about two thousand horse.[21]

"XXII.41. But even Fortune furnished material to the recklessness and over-hasty temper of the consul. The repulse of a foraging party had led to a general mellay, which came about from the soldiers rushing forward to attack the enemy, rather than from any plan or orders on the part of the generals; and in this the Phoenicians by no means held their own. [2] About seventeen hundred of them were slain and not more than a hundred of Romans and allies. But the consul Paulus, who was in command that day —for they commanded on alternate days —was [3] fearful of an ambuscade and checked the victors in their headlong pursuit, despite the angry remonstrances of Varro, who cried out that they had let the enemy slip through their hands and that they might have brought the war to a conclusion if they had not relaxed their efforts. [4] Hannibal was not greatly disconcerted by this reverse; indeed he rejoiced that the hook should have been baited, as it were, for the rashness of the more impetuous consul, and especially for that of the new soldiers. [5] All the circumstances of his enemies were as familiar to him as his own: that their generals were unlike each other and were at loggerheads, and that nearly two-thirds of their army consisted of recruits. [6] Believing, therefore, that place and time were favourable for a ruse, he left his camp full of every sort of public and of private riches, and putting himself at the head of his troops, who carried nothing but their weapons, marched over the nearest ridge, drew up the [7] infantry in ambush on the left, and the cavalry on the right, and made the baggage-train pass

21   See Polybius II, *Histories*, Books 3-4 (Translation of William R. Paton; Loeb Classical Library; Cambridge, Harvard University Press 1922).

▲ Aerial view of Cannae city and battlefield.

through the valley between, intending to fall upon [8] the enemy whilst they were preoccupied and encumbered with the pillage of the camp, which would seem to them to have been deserted by its owners. [9] He left a large number of fires burning, as though he had sought by means of this illusory appearance of an encampment to hold the consuls to their positions —as he had cheated Fabius the year before —till he could gain as long a start as possible in his retreat. 42. When day came, first the fact that the outposts had been withdrawn, and afterwards —as they came nearer —the unwonted silence filled the Romans with amazement. [2] Then, as it became quite evident that there was no one in the camp, there was a rush of men to the headquarters of the consuls, announcing that the enemy had retreated in such trepidation as to quit the camp without striking their tents, and had even left a great number of fires burning to conceal their flight. [3] Next they began to clamour for the order to advance and to pursue the enemy and plunder the camp without delay, and one of the consuls behaved like a member of the mob of soldiers. [4] Paulus kept insisting on the need for watchfulness and circumspection, and finally, when there was no other way in which he could withstand the mutiny and the leader of the mutiny, he sent the praefect Marius Statilius with a troop of Lucanian horse to reconnoitre. [5] Riding up to the gates, Statilius commanded the others to wait outside the trenches, and himself with two horsemen entered the camp. After making a thorough and careful examination he reported that¹ there was undoubtedly some treachery afoot. [6] The fires, he said, had been left on the side of the camp that faced the Romans; the tents were open and all kinds of valuables were left exposed to view; here and there he had seen silver carelessly flung down in the lanes, as if to tempt a pillager.[7] The report, which had been made with the purpose of checking the soldiers' greed, only inflamed it, and they began to shout that if the signal were not given, they would go without any leaders. But there was no lack of a leader; for Varro at once gave the command to start. [8] Paulus himself wished to delay; and when the sacred fowls had refused their sanction,³ he gave orders to notify his colleague, who was just setting forth with the standards from [9] the gate. Varro was greatly vexed at this, but the recent disaster of

Flaminius and the memorable defeat at sea of the consul Claudius, in the first Punic War made him fearful of offending the [10] heavenly powers. On that day, it might almost be said, the very gods put off, but did not prevent, the calamity that impended over the Romans: for it chanced that when the consul ordered the standards back into the camp and the soldiers were refusing to obey him, two slaves appeared on the scene, one belonging to a Formian, the other to a Sidicinian knight. They had been captured by the Numidians, along with other foragers, in the consulship of Servilius and Atilius, and on that day had escaped back to [11] their masters. Being conducted to the consuls, they stated that Hannibal's entire army was lying in ambush just over the [12] nearest hills. Their opportune arrival restored the authority of the consuls, when one of them, by running after popularity, and by unprincipled indulgence, had impaired their prestige —beginning with his own —amongst the soldiers. 43. Hannibal, perceiving that the Romans, although they had acted ill-advisedly, had not proceeded to the extremity of rashness, returned to the camp, his stratagem having been detected and rendered idle. [2] There, however, the scarcity of corn forbade his remaining many days, and new plans were daily forming, not only amongst the soldiers, the mingled offscourings of every race on earth, but even in the mind of the general himself. [3] For when the men, with murmurs at first and afterwards with loud clamours, demanded their arrears of pay, and complained at first of the scarcity of corn, and finally of being starved; and when the report went round that the mercenaries —particularly those of Spanish blood —had resolved on going over to the enemy; [4] they say that even Hannibal himself had thoughts of abandoning all his infantry and saving himself and his cavalry by escaping into Gaul. [5] Such being the projects that were entertained in camp and such the temper of his soldiers, he decided to move from his present quarters to Apulia,1 where the climate was warmer and in consequence of this the harvest earlier; at the same time it would be the more difficult, the greater their distance from the enemy, for those of his followers who were fickle to desert. [6] He set out in the night, after making up some fires, as before, and leaving a few tents standing where they would be seen, so that the Romans might be withheld from following him through fear of an ambush, as before. But when the same Lucanian, Statilius, had made a thorough reconnaissance beyond the camp and on the other side of the mountains, and had reported seeing the enemy on the march a long way off, then the question of pursuing him began to be [8] debated. The consuls were each of the same mind as they had always been; but Varro had the support of almost everybody, Paulus of none except Servilius, the consul of the year [9] before. The will of the majority prevailed, and they set forward, under the urge of destiny, to make

---

E – Hastatus or Princeps

This figure wears a red tunic and *caligae*, hobnailed sandals. His head is protected by a bronze Montefortino. His armor consists in a *cardiophylax*, or *spongia pectoris*, a simple breastplate and backplate in bronze, which covers the hart and the central part of the abdomen. These breastplates characterized the defensive weaponry of the Hill Peoples, and were quite similar to the Etruscan discs. The earliest example comes from the Capestrano Warrior. Here, the abdominal plate is probably of Campanian origin, and it is clearly inspired by a muscle cuirass. The plates, which were made of bronze with iron backing, were joined by a hinged shoulder strap. Besides, two leather straps, which pass under the arms, hold the two plates in place over his abdomen. Polybius, relates that breast and back plates were still in use in the second century BCE Roman army. Contrary to the *veles*, this *hastatus* or princeps is armed with a heavy pilum. *Pila* were divided in heavy, as this one, and light *pila*, as the one in the previous plate. The *pilum*, a javelin, was introduced in the fourth century BCE, possibly by the Etruscans. Its length varied from 0.15 m to 1.2 m in length. The wooden shaft was covered by an iron shank with a pyramidal head. This could be joined to the shaft by a socket, the first type, or by a flat tang, secured with one or two rivets, the second type. The point was often barbed. The heavy *pilum* was used to pierce the enemy's shield, rendering it useless, and sometimes wounding the man behind it, often disrupting the enemy formation. The lighter *pilum*, the shorter flat tanged type was used primarily as a counter siege weapon. His weapons also include the heavy oval shield, or *scutum*, and the long *gladius hispaniensis*.

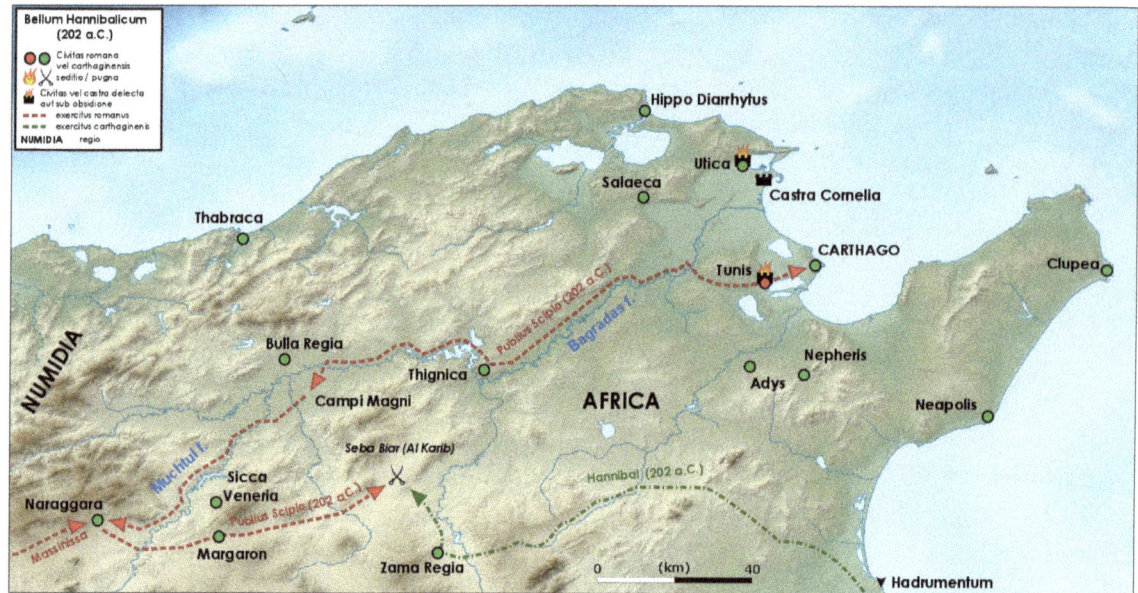

▲ Scipio's African campaign

Cannae famous for the calamity which there befell the [10] Romans. This was the village near which Hannibal had pitched his camp, with his back to the Volturnus, a wind that brings clouds of dust over the drought-parched [11] plains. Such a disposition was very convenient for the camp itself and bound to be particularly salutary when the troops formed up for battle, facing in the opposite direction, with the wind blowing only on their backs, and ready to6 fight with enemies half-blinded by the dust driven into their faces. 44. The consuls, after making a sufficient reconnaissance of the roads, followed the Phoenicians until they came to Cannae, where, having the enemy in view, they divided their forces, as they had done before, and fortified two camps, at about the same distance from one another as at Gereonium. [2] The river Aufidus, flowing past both their camps, was readily accessible to water-carriers at such spots as were convenient for each, though not without fighting; [3] it was, however, from the smaller camp, which was situated across the Aufidus, that the Romans could fetch water more freely, since the enemy had no troops posted on the further bank.[4] Hannibal had conceived a hope that the consuls would give him an opportunity of fighting in a place that was formed by nature for a cavalry action, in which arm he was invincible. He therefore drew out his men in battle array and ordered the Numidians to make a sally and provoke the enemy. [5] This caused the camp of the Romans to be once more the scene of strife amongst the soldiers and dissension between the consuls. Paulus cast in Varro's teeth the recklessness of Sempronius and Flaminius; [6] Varro retorted that Fabius was a specious example for timid and slothful generals, and called on gods and men to witness that it was through no fault of his that Hannibal had by now acquired as it were a prescriptive right to Italy, for he was kept in fetters by his colleague, and the soldiers, enraged as they were and eager to fight, were deprived of swords and arms. [7] Paulus rejoined that if anything untoward should befall the legions, recklessly abandoned to an ill-advised and rash engagement, he would himself be guiltless of all blame, but would share in all the consequences; let Varro, he said, see to it, that where tongues were bold and ready, hands —when it came to fighting —were no less so. 45. While they wasted time, rather quarrelling than consulting, Hannibal withdrew the rest of his troops, whom he had kept in line till far on in the day, [2] into his camp, and sent the Numidians across the river to attack the men from the smaller Roman camp who were fetching water. [3] They had hardly come out upon the other bank when their shouts and tumult sent that unorganized rabble flying, and they rode on till they came to the party that was stationed in front of the rampart, and almost to the very gates. [4] So wholly outrageous, however, did it seem that by now even a Roman camp should be terrorized by irregular auxiliaries, that only one thing kept the Romans from crossing the river forthwith and giving battle —the fact that Paulus happened then to be in command.[5] The next morning, therefore, Varro, whom the lot had made commander for that day, hung out the signal, without saying a word of the matter to his colleague, and, making his troops fall in, led them over the river. Paulus followed him, for he could more easily disapprove the plan than deprive it of his help. [6] Once across, they joined to their own the forces which they had kept in the smaller camp, and marshalled their battle-line as follows: on the right wing —the one nearer the river —they placed the Roman cavalry, and next them the Roman foot; [7] the left wing had on the outside the cavalry of the allies; and nearer the centre, in contact with the Roman legions, the infantry of the allies. The slingers and other light-armed auxiliaries were formed up in front. [8] The consuls had charge of the wings, Terentius of the left, Aemilius of the right; and Geminus Servilius was entrusted with the centre. 46. Hannibal crossed the river at break of day, after sending ahead of him the Baliares and the other light-armed troops, and posted each corps in line of battle, in the order in which he had brought it over. [2] The Gallic and Spanish horse were next the river, on the left wing, facing the Roman cavalry; [3] the right wing was assigned to the Numidian horse; the centre was composed of infantry, so arranged as to have the Africans at both ends, and between them Gauls and Spaniards. [4] The Africans might have passed for an array of Romans, equipped as they were with arms captured partly at the Trebia but mostly at Lake Trasumennus. [5] The Gauls

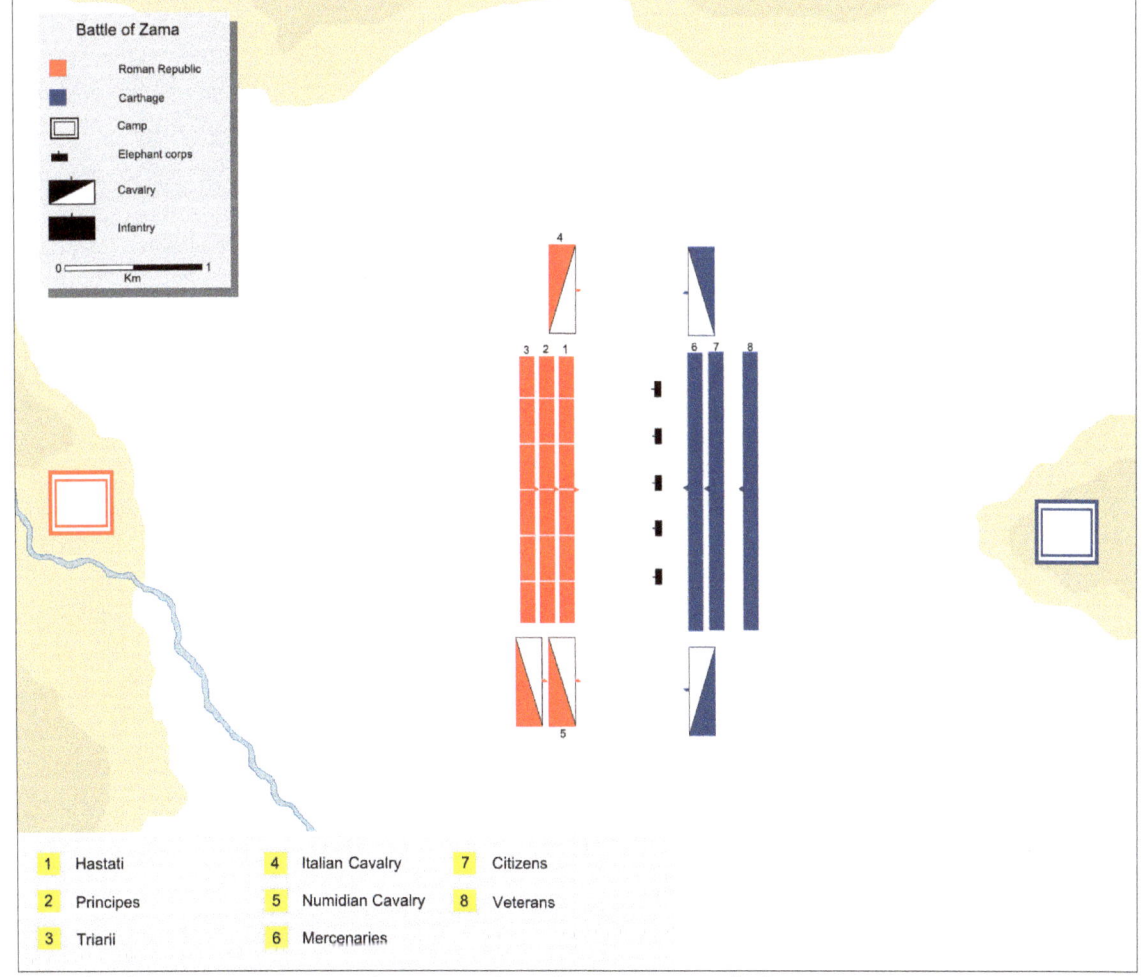

▲ Battle of Zama, 202 BCE – Initial Roman and Carthaginian armies' deployment.

and the Spaniards had shields of almost the same shape; their swords were different in use and in appearance, those of the Gauls being very long and pointless, whilst the Spaniards, who attacked as a rule more by thrusting than by striking, had pointed ones that were short and handy.1 These tribes were more terrifying to look on than the others, because of the size of their bodies and the display they made of them. [6] The Gauls were naked from the navel up; the Spaniards had formed up wearing crimson-bordered linen tunics that shone with a dazzling whiteness. The total number of the infantry who then took their place in line was forty thousand, of the cavalry ten thousand. [7] The generals commanding on the wings were Hasdrubal on the left, Maharbal on the right; Hannibal himself, with his brother Mago, had the centre. [8] The sun —whether they had so placed themselves on purpose or stood as they did by accident —was, very conveniently for both sides, on their flanks, the Romans looking south, the Phoenicians north. [9] A wind —which those who live in those parts call Volturnus —beginning to blow against the Romans carried clouds of dust right into their faces and prevented them from seeing anything. 47. With a shout the auxiliaries rushed forward and the battle began between the light-armed troops. Then the Gallic and Spanish horse which formed the left wing engaged with the Roman right in a combat very unlike a cavalry action. [2] For they had to charge front to front, there being no room to move out round the flank, for the river shut them in on one side and the ranks of infantry on the other. [3] Both parties pushed straight ahead, and as the horses came to a standstill, packed together in the throng, the riders began to grapple with their enemies and drag them from their seats. They were fighting on foot now, for the most part; but sharp though the struggle was, it was soon over, and the defeated Roman cavalry turned and fled. [4] Towards the end of the cavalry engagement the infantry got into action. At first they were evenly matched in strength and courage, as long as the Gauls and Spaniards maintained their ranks; [5] but at last the Romans, by prolonged and frequent efforts, pushing forward with an even front and a dense line, drove in the wedge-like formation which projected from the enemy's line, for it was too thin to be strong; [6] and then, as the Gauls and Span-

---

F – Triarius

This figure wears a red tunic and *caligae*, hobnailed sandals. His head is protected by an iron Attic helmet with cheekpieces, topped by a central crest of horse hair and two side feathers. He is defended by a *lorica hamata*, with underneath a *subarmalis* ending in leather *pteryges*. His main defensive weapon is the enormous *scutum*. Slightly curved inward, it could reach a height of 1.2 m. Polybius narrates that it was made of two sheets of wood glued together and covered, first with canvas, and then, with skin. The scutum could have a metal frame, as protection against slashing weapons. The *scutum* had a spindle shaped boss and a long outer spine. The center of the boss is hallowed out to allow the hand to grasp the handle. A similar example had been found in Egypt at Kasr El Harit in the Fayum region. Although the archaeologist as Celtic it is probably Roman. These shields are depicted on the reliefs of the monument of Aemilius Paullus at Delphi, on the altar of Domitius Ahenobarbus, and on reliefs from the Temple of Athena, at Pergamum. A short greave defends the lower part of the left leg. He is armed with a spear and with the *gladius hispaniensis*. This iron sword was characterized by a straight blade that could reach the length of 65 cm. Polybius states that "it has an excellent point and a strong cutting edge on both sides, as its blade is firm and reliable" (Polybius, Histories VI.23.6-7). The handle was wooden made, sometimes overlaid in bronze or plated with silver. The handle was characterized by four identical grooves that gave a much better grip. The main purpose of the pommel, set at the end of the handle, hemispherical or trilobate shaped, was to give to the sword the necessary balance to slash with greater strength. Livy, while describing an engagement of Roman legionaries against Macedonian phalangist, narrated that "Macedonian soldiers" being accustomed to fight with the Greeks and Illyrians, had seen the wounds which were made by spears and arrows and, on rare occasions, by lance; but now they saw bodies mutilated by the Spanish sword, arms lopped off at the shoulder, or heads separated from bodies with the neck cut right through, or entrails lying open, and other repulsive wounds, and there was general panic as they began to see what sort of weapon and what sort of men they had to fight. (Livy, *Roman History* XXXI.34).

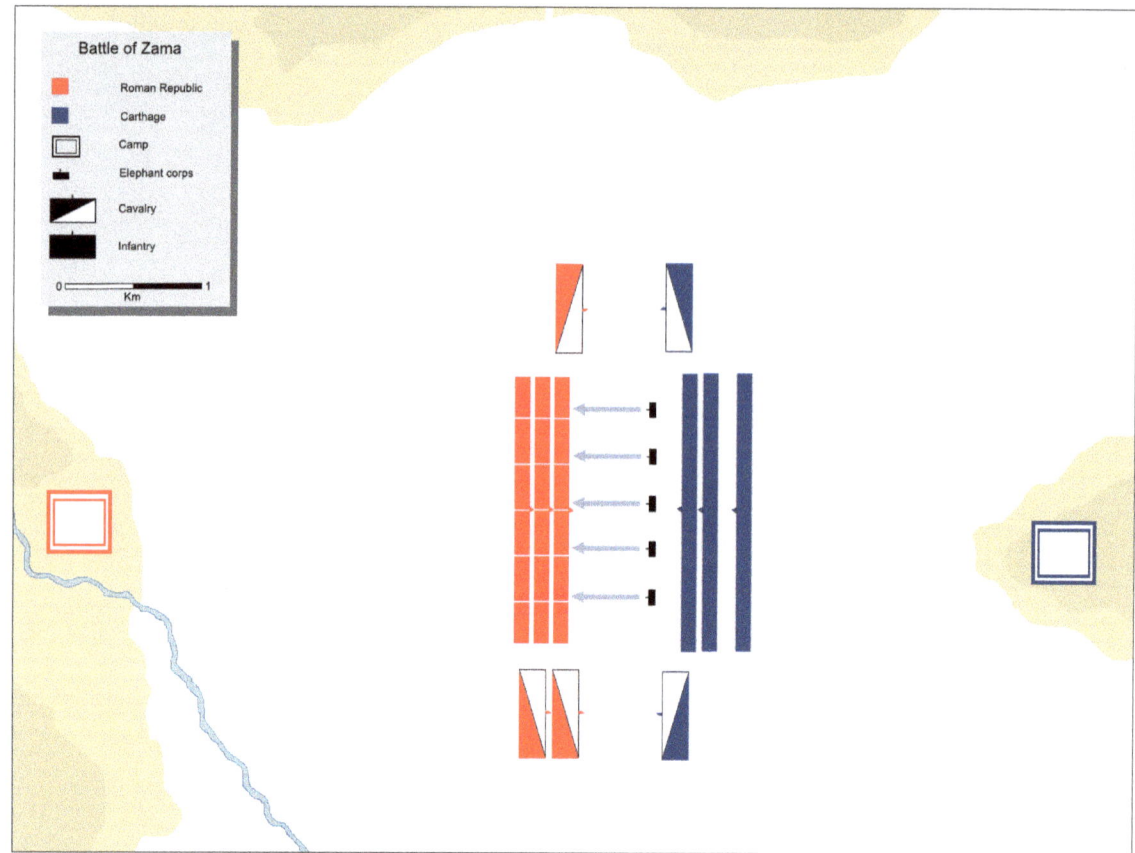

▲ Battle of Zama, 202 BCE – Hannibal elephants' charge; the panicked elephants turn on the Carthaginian left wing rampaging through it.

iards gave way and fell back in confusion, pressed forward and without once stopping forced their way through the crowd of fleeing, panic-stricken foes, till they reached first the centre and ultimately —for they met with no resistance —the African supports. [7] These had been used to form the two wings, which had been drawn back, while the centre, where the Gauls and Spaniards had been stationed, projected somewhat. When this wedge was first driven back so far as to straighten the front, and then, continuing to yield, even left a hollow in the centre, the Africans had already begun a flanking movement on either side, and as the Romans rushed incautiously in between, they [8] enveloped them, and presently, extending their wings, crescent-wise, even closed in on their rear. [9] From this moment the Romans, who had gained one battle to no purpose, gave over the pursuit and slaughter of the Gauls and Spaniards and began a new fight with [10] the Africans. In this they were at a twofold disadvantage: they were shut in, while their enemies ranged on every side of them; they were tired, and faced troops that were fresh and strong. 48. By this time the Roman left, where the cavalry of the allies had taken position facing the Numidians, was also engaged, though the fighting was at first but sluggish. It began with a Punic ruse. [2] About five hundred Numidians, who, in addition to their customary arms and missiles, carried swords concealed under their corslets, pretended to desert. [3] Riding over from their own side, with their bucklers at their backs, they suddenly dismounted and threw down bucklers and javelins at the feet of their enemies. Being received into the midst of their ranks they were conducted to the rear and ordered to fall in behind. [4] And while the battle was getting under way at every point, they kept quite still; but no sooner were the minds and eyes of all absorbed in the struggle, than they snatched up the shields which lay strewn about everywhere amongst the heaps of slain, and

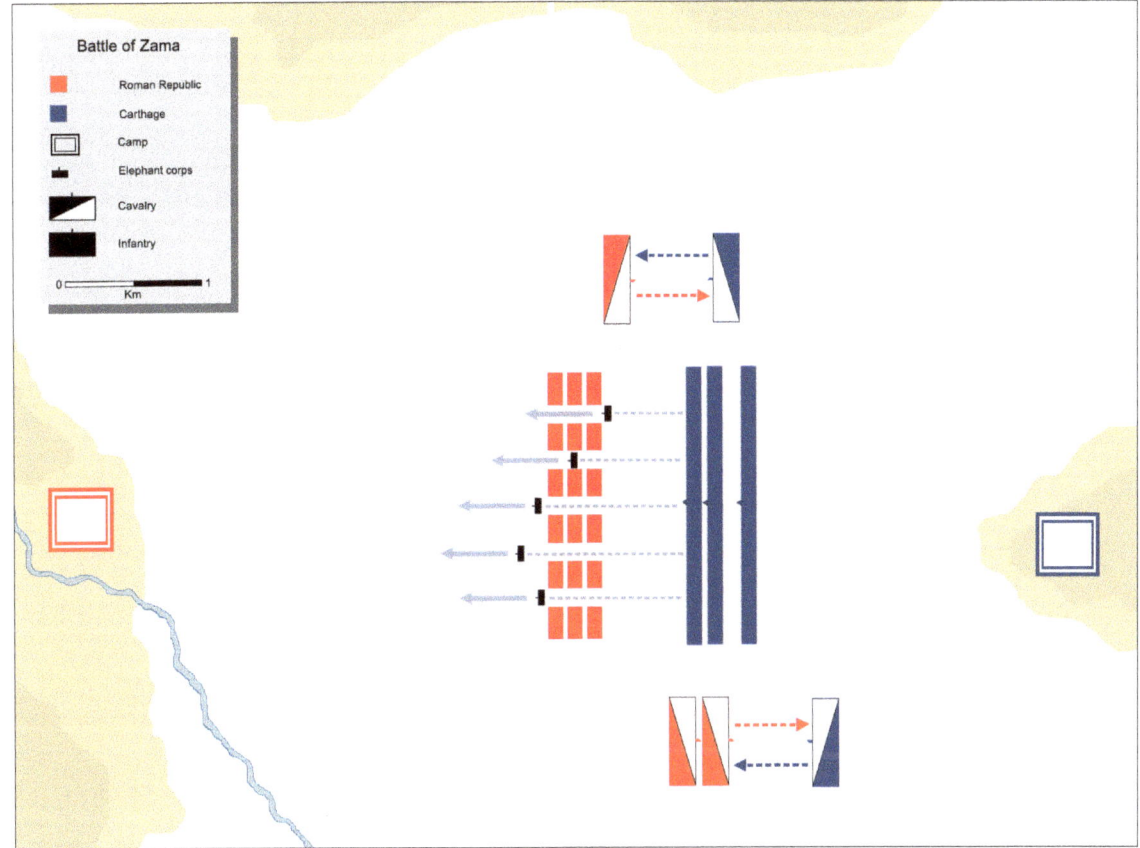

▲ Battle of Zama, 202 BCE – The Roman right wing defeats the Carthaginian cavalry, while the Roman left-wing outmaneuvers the Carthaginian right wing; the remaining elephants are enticed through the lanes and slain.

assailing the Romans from behind and striking at their backs and hamstrings, effected a great slaughter and a terror and confusion that were even greater. [5] And now in one place there was a panic rout and in another an obstinate though hopeless struggle, when Hasdrubal, who commanded in that part of the field, withdrew the Numidians from the centre —since they fought but half-heartedly against men who met them face to face —and [6] dispatching them in pursuit of the scattered fugitives, sent in the Spanish and Gallic cavalry to help the Africans, who were now almost exhausted, though more with slaying than with fighting. 49. In the other part of the field Paulus, although he had received a severe wound from a sling at [2] the very outset of the battle, nevertheless repeatedly opposed himself to Hannibal, with his men in close formation, and at several points restored the [3] fight. He was guarded by Roman cavalry, who finally let their horses go, as the consul was growing too weak even to control his horse. At this Hannibal, being told by someone that the consul had ordered his troopers to dismount, is said to have exclaimed: "How much better if he had handed them over to me in [4] fetters!" The dismounted horsemen fought as men no longer doubting that the enemy must be [5] victorious. They were beaten, but chose rather to die where they stood than to run away; and the victors, angry that their victory was thus delayed, cut them down, when they could not rout them. But they routed them at last, when only a few were left, exhausted with fighting and with [6] wounds. The survivors were now all dispersed, and those who could attempted to regain their horses and escape. [7] Gnaeus Lentulus, a tribune of the soldiers, as he rode by on his horse, caught sight of the consul sitting on a stone and covered with [8] blood. "Lucius Aemilius," he cried, "on whom the gods ought to look down in mercy, as the only man without guilt in this day's disaster, take this horse, while you have still a little strength remaining and I can attend you and raise you up and guard [9] you. Make not this battle calamitous by a consul's death; even without that there are tears and grief enough. "To this the consul answered, "All honour, Cornelius, to your [10] manhood! But waste not in unavailing pity the little time you have to escape the enemy. Go, and tell the senators in public session to fortify the City of Rome and garrison it strongly before the victorious enemy draws near: in private say to Quintus Fabius that Lucius Aemilius has lived till this hour and now dies remembering his [11] precepts. As for me, let me breathe my last in the midst of my slaughtered soldiers, lest either for a second time I be brought to trial after being consul, or else stand forth the accuser of my colleague, blaming another in defence of my own [12] innocence." While they were speaking, there came up with them first a crowd of fleeing Romans, and then the enemy, who overwhelmed the consul, without knowing who he was, beneath a rain of [13] missiles. Lentulus, thanks to his horse, escaped in the confusion. The rout was now everywhere complete. Seven thousand men escaped into the smaller camp, ten thousand into the larger, and about two thousand into the village of Cannae [14] itself. These last were immediately cut off by Carthalo and his cavalry, for the village was not fortified. The other consul, whether by accident or by design, had not joined any throng of fugitives, but fled to Venusia with some fifty [15] horsemen. It is said that forty-five thousand five hundred foot and two thousand seven hundred horse were slain, in an almost equal proportion of citizens and [16] allies. In the number were the quaestors of both consuls, Lucius Atilius and Lucius Furius Bibaculus, and twenty-nine military tribunes, some of consular rank, some of *praetor*ian or aedilician —amongst others are mentioned Gnaeus Servilius Geminus and Marcus Minucius, who had been master of the horse in the preceding years and consul several years before [17] —and besides these, eighty senators or men who had held offices which would have given them the right to be elected to the senate, but had volunteered to serve as soldiers in the [18] legions. The prisoners taken in this battle are said to have numbered three thousand foot-soldiers and fifteen hundred horsemen. 50. Such was the battle of Cannae, a calamity as memorable as that suffered at the Allia, and though less grave in its results —because [2] the enemy failed to follow up his victory —yet for the slaughter of the army even more grievous and disgraceful. [3] For the flight at the Allia, though it betrayed the City, saved the army: at Cannae the consul who fled was accompanied by a scant fifty men; the other, dying, had well-nigh the entire army with him. In the two Roman camps the crowd was half-armed and destitute of leaders. The men in the larger camp sent a messenger bidding those in the smaller one come over to them in the night, while the enemy, exhausted by the fighting and by the feasting that had followed on [4] their triumph, were sunk in sleep: they would then set out in one body for Canusium. [5] This plan some were for totally rejecting. Why, they asked, did not those who summoned them come themselves to the smaller camp, where they could just as well effect a junction? Clearly because the ground between was covered with enemies and they preferred to expose to such danger the persons of others rather than their own. Some were not so much displeased with the plan as wanting in resolution. [6] Then said the military tribune Publius Sempronius Tuditanus: "So

---

G – Veles and Triarius waiting for the onslaught

The figure on the left, a *veles*, wears a white tunic and *caligae*. His head is protected by a simple Montefortino, covered by a wolf head skin. He is defended by a parma in his left hand. He had already thrown his two light *pila* at the enemy. Thus, once unsheathed his sword, he is ready to give a good fight.

The figure on the right, a *triarius*, wears a red tunic and *caligae*. His head is protected by an iron Attic helmet with cheekpieces, topped by a central crest of horse hair and two side feathers. He is defended by a lorica hamata, with underneath a *subarmalis* ending in leather *pteryges*. He is defended by a *scutum*. He is armed with a spear and with the *gladius hispaniensis*. By now, he is crouched behind the heavy oval shield, and thrusting outward his spear, waiting for the final onslaught. Yes, as it was said, res ad *triarios venit*, the heat of the battle had reached the *triarii*. Our soldier, in other words, shall carry on fighting to the bitter end.

1

2

you had rather be captured by the greediest and most cruel of foes, and be appraised at so much a head by those who ask, 'Are you a Roman citizen or a Latin ally?' in order that from the insults and misery you suffer, the other may win distinction? [7] 'Not so!' each man will answer, if you are indeed fellow citizens of Lucius Aemilius the consul, who preferred an honourable death to life with ignominy, and of all those heroes who lie in heaps around him! [8] But before daylight surprises us and the enemy blocks our way in greater force, let us break out through these men that are clamouring in disorder and confusion at our gates. [9] With a sword and a stout heart a man may pass through enemies, be they never so thick. In close formation4 you may scatter this loose and unorganized force as though there were nothing in your way. Follow me, then, as many of you as desire safety for yourselves and for the commonwealth! [10] "Uttering these words he grasped his sword, and, forming a column, strode away through the midst of the enemy; [11] and when the Numidians hurled missiles at their right sides, which were unprotected, they shifted their shields to the right and so got through, about six hundred of them, to the larger camp; and thence, after being joined by the other great body of men, they made their way at once without loss to Canusium. [12] These things the conquered did rather from the urge of such courage as each derived from his own nature or from chance than in consequence of their own deliberation or any man's authority.[22] The casualties were enormous. Polybius and Livy are quite dramatic in the description of the aftermath of the battle. Polybius narrates that only 70 Roman cavalrymen escaped to Venusia with Varro, while only 3000 cavalrymen from the allied contingent found refuge in neighboring cities, divided in scattered groups. Of the infantry, only 3000 got away to the neighboring towns. Circa 10.000 infantrymen were captured fighting, although they were part of Lucius Aemilius Paulus reserve and only 3000 got away from the field (Polybius, *Histories* III, 117). The succeeding part of Polybius account is missing. Thus, in this case the data that can be collected from the account of Polybius is quite useless. According to Livy the disordered flight brought back 7000 men in the minor camp, 10.000 in the main camp, and around 2000 men in the same village of Cannae, who were immediately surrounded by Cartalo and his cavalry. Varro fled to Venosa with 50 cavalrymen. The casualties amounted to 45.500 infantrymen and 2700 cavalrymen, in the same quantity Romans and the Italic contingent (Livy, *History of Rome* XXII, 49).

But, there were also survivors. According to Livy, the survivors in the two camps got organized. The first group of the survivors from the minor camp, according to Livy only 600 men, joined those in the main camp, planning to escape in the direction of Canosa. Under the command of the tribune P. Sempronius Tuditanus, the survivors got organized, and although facing the attacks of the hostile Numidian cavalry, arrived at Canosa (Livy, *History of Rome* XXII 50-56). According to Connolly, of the survivors of the battle, circa 7000 Roman fell in Hannibal hands. Circa 10.000 men succeeded in escaping to Canosa, where they joined the consul Terentius Varro. Later on, Hannibal released without ransom a similar number of soldiers from the Italic contingent. This would bring the total number of survivors to 25.000. Thus, all the 10.000 survivors from the main camp survived, together with a good part from the minor camp, that included the 600 men and what Livy calls *alio magno agmine*. Thus, most of the men in both camps survived, Romans as well as allies. Goldsworthy, on the other hand, argues that most of the Roman soldiers in both camps, roughly 17.000, surrendered. Only 10.000 men survived the battle.[23]

---

22   Livy V, *The History of Rome*, Books 21-22 (Translation of Benjamin O. Foster; Loeb Classical Library; Cambridge, Harvard University Press 1929).

23   See P. Connolly, *Greece and Rome at War*, London 1981, p. 188. See for a different opinion A. Goldsworthy, *The Fall of Carthage, The Punic Wars 265-146 BC*, London 2003, pp. 213-214 on the Roman losses at Cannae. According to Caven there were 10.000/15.000 survivors. See B. Caven, *The Punic Wars*, London 1980, p. 152.

D. 216-215 BCE: THE CREATION OF THE *LEGIONES CANNENSES*

Which were the surviving legions, which were later amalgamated together in the so-called *legiones cannenses*? According to Livy only four military tribunes arrived at Canosa, the tribune of the 1st legion Fabius Maximus, son of the *dictator*, those of the 2nd legion L. Publicius Bibulus and P. Cornelius Scipio, and Appius Claudius Pulcher tribunus of the 3rd legion. Besides, Livy narrates that both Publius Cornelius Scipio and Appius Claudius were given command of the survivors (Livy, *History of Rome* XXII, 53). Livy mentions the 1st, 2nd, and 3rd legions. Evidently Livy numbers the first three of the eight legions present at Cannae from 1st to 8th. However, at first sight it is impossible to know which number given by Livy corresponds to which legion (1st, 2nd, 12th, 13th, 14th, 15th, 16th and 17th). However, Livy states clearly that at Ticinum, Publius Cornelius Scipio, a *tribunus* of the 1st or 2nd legion, as Livy does not go into details, saved the life of his father. But now, the same Publius Cornelius Scipio was still as *tribunus militum* of the 2nd legion. Probably, the 2nd legion of Livy was the 2nd legion once commanded by the father of Publius Cornelius Scipio, levied in 218 BCE. Evidently, the young Publius Cornelius Scipio continued to perform as military tribune in the same legion. It is also quite possible that also the 1st legion, whose *tribunus*, mentioned by Livy, was Fabius Maximus, the son of the *dictator*, corresponded to the 1st legion also levied by the father of Publius Cornelius Scipio in 218 BCE. Thus, the number given by Livy to the legions present at Cannae does correspond to their veteran status. The 1st and 2nd legions of Publius Cornelius Scipio were the most veteran legions, and, therefore, received the first two numerals. Probably the 3rd legion was one of the two legions levied by Geminus, the 12th or the 13th.

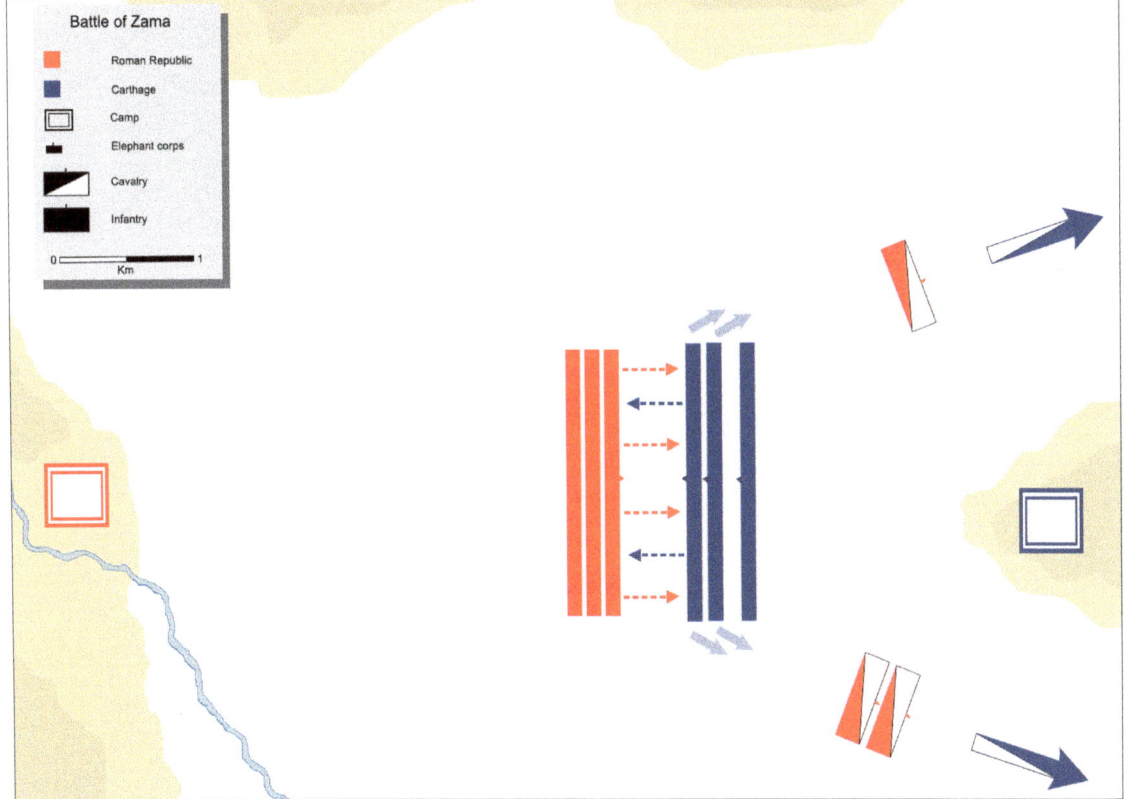

▲ Battle of Zama, 202 BCE – The Carthaginian cavalry is routed off the field; Scipio defeats Hannibal's first and second lines of infantry.

1

2

The fate of the four officers mentioned by Livy indeed is parallel to that of the majority of the surviving soldiers. Probably, if the tribunes were no cowards, (and according to Livy they were not), they saved themselves together with their own soldiers, each tribune commanding soldiers from his own legion. Thus, most of the survivors came from the two legions of Scipio levied in 218 BCE, and from one of the legions levied by Geminus in 217 BCE. All these legions had a better military training and experience than the four legions levied by the *dictator* Quintus Fabius Maximus. It is probable, thus, that if a majority of the survivors came from a specific legion or legions, these would have been the ones mentioned.

In the immediate aftermath of the battle of Cannae, the two *legiones cannenses* were sent to Canusium (Canosa) under the command of Claudius Marcellus, who was then the *praetor* in command of the fleet at Ostia (Livy, *History of Rome* XXII, 57). Moreover, the sailors serving in the Ostia Fleet were formed in a legion and they were sent to Teanum Sidicinum to reinforce Marcellus's new command. This consisted in the two *legiones cannenses*. Livy narrated that this legion formed by sailors was the 3rd. Maybe the number 3rd indicates that this legion was the third legion after the two Cannae Legions, the 1st and 2nd, available in the area. Afterwards, the Senate appointed once more a *dictator*, Marcus Junius Pera, together with his *magister equitum*, Sempronius Gracchus. The *dictator* levied four more legions, the 22nd, 23rd, 24th, 25th legions, two legions of volunteer slaves, and a force of 6000 paroled criminals (Livy, *History of Rome* XXII, 57). The Roman Republic was in a terrible situation, if, according to Livy, this time the levied were seventeen years old, and they were still wearing the toga praetexta (Livy, *History of Rome* XXIII, 13). And yet, by the end of 216 BCE, the Roman Republic could field 25.000 men.[24] After the desertion of Capua the two *legiones cannenses* and the legion of marines under the command of Marcellus were sent to the Casilinum area at Suessula (Livy, *History of Rome* XXIII, 2-10).[25] The *dictator* Marcus Junius Pera joined later Marcellus with the 20th and 21st and the 6000 paroled criminals. The task of Marcellus was to relieve Nola, which was in territory held by the Carthaginians. His army was successful in a skirmish in front of Nola's walls (Livy, *History of Rome* XXIII, 16). Then, Marcellus successful retired for winter quarters at Suessula. Thus, the two *legiones cannenses* continued to fight, maintaining their legal status of citizen soldiers for a full year after the battle of Cannae. Only later in 215 BCE after the election of the two *consules suffecti* Marcus Claudius Marcellus and Quintus Fabius Maximus, after the death of the consul Lucius Postumius Albinus, in the second part of the year, the Senate deliberated on the status of the two *legiones cannenses* (Livy, *History of Rome* XXIII, 24), already discussed.

---

24   See A. Goldsworthy, *The Fall of Carthage, The Punic Wars 265-146 BC*, London 2003, pp. 219-220.
25   See A. F. Lazenby, *Hannibal's War, A Military History of the Second Punic War*, Warminster 1978, p. 91.

H – Hastatus, or princeps, and Triarius

The figure on the left, an *hastatus* or *princeps*, wears a red tunic and *caligae* sandals. His head is protected by a bronze Montefortino. His armor consists in a simple *cardiophylax*, or *spongia pectoris*. He is armed with a heavy *pilum*. His weapons also include the heavy oval shield, or *scutum*, and the long *gladius hispaniensis*.

The figure on the right, a *triarius*, wears a red tunic and *caligae*. His head is protected by bronze Montefortino with cheekpieces. He is defended by a *lorica hamata*, which reaches his hips. The shoulder guards, U shaped, are made in linen. As in a *linothorax*, the linen corselet, various layers of linen were glued together. He is defended by a *scutum*. He is armed with a spear and with the *gladius hispaniensis*.

In the aftermath of the *senatus consultum*, the two *legiones cannenses*, as well as the Italic contingent, were sent to Sicily in garrison duty under the command of the *praetor* Appius Claudius Pulcher, by Titus Mecilius Croto (Livy, *History of Rome* XXIII, 31). Instead, the legions that garrisoned Sicily were sent back to the battlefields of Campania.

It seemed that the *legiones cannenses* would finish the war ingloriously in Sicily in garrison duty, without taking part in any more military action. It was not to be. The situation in Sicily soon deteriorated. In late 216 or early 215 BCE the old Hiero, tyrant of Syracuse, and a staunch supporter of Rome died. Hiero was succeeded by his son Hieronymus. The new ruler, very young, was inexperienced. He only sensed that the situation was bad for the Romans. He, thus, began to negotiate with Hannibal. His purpose was to evict the Romans from Sicily, and share the government on the island with the Carthaginians. The *praetor* Appius Claudius Pulcher, who governed Sicily, failed to stop Hieronymus. However, Hieronymus was soon murdered. New magistrates were elected, between them, the exiles Hippocrates and Epycles, who came from Carthage. The Syracusans sent Hippocrates to garrison Leontini. Hippocrates declared the city independent and began to raid the Roman province.

When the Greek city of Syracuse, rebelled to the Romans, the only forces that Rome had in Sicily at the time were the two *legiones cannenses*. According to Lazenby, Rome immediately utilized the two legions to stem the tide. In fact, the two legions were the only military force available to the *praetor* Appius Claudis Pulcher.[26] However, the *praetor* did not begin the military operations, but waited for the new elected consul till the end of 214 BCE. In the year 214 BCE, the two consuls elected were Quintus Fabius Maximus, the *cunctator* of 216 BCE and Marcus Claudius Marcellus (Livy, *History of Rome* XXIV, 9).

In the year 214 BCE, the Romans had between fourteen or twenty legions, of whom four were levied at the beginning of the year by the two consuls (Livy, *History of Rome* XXIV, 11). According to Livy in the year 214 BCE the Roman army consisted in two legions garrisoned Cisalpine Gaul, two legions in Sardinia, and two in Sicily (the two *legiones cannenses*). Quintus Fabius, son of the *cunctator*, *praetor* in Apulia, had two legions (20th and 21st); Tiberius Gracchus commanded the two slave legions levied in 216 BCE after Cannae. One legion was in the Picenum with the *proconsul* Terentius Varo the defeated consul at Cannae, a legion was commanded by Marcus Valerius and consisted in the marines of the Brindisi fleet. Two legions, or *legiones urbanae*, remained at Rome. Six more legions were levied at Rome by the two consuls, the 26th, 27th, 28th, 29th, 30th and 31st. However, the total of legions under arms was twenty. Marcellus joined the operations in Campania with the 22nd and 23rd legions. However, Livy did not account as legions the two slave legions, or that the consuls levied only four legions. Modern scholars disagree on the total number of the legions. While for Connolly in 214 BCE the Romans had twenty legions, according to De Sanctis and Toynbee there were no less than twenty legions in 214 BCE.[27]

Sicily was assigned to the *praetor* Publius Cornelius Lentulus (Livy, *History of Rome* XXIV, 9-10). Marcellus did not immediately come to Sicily, but for a good part of the year, he continued to fight against Hannibal in Campania together with the other consul and Tiberius Gracchus (Livy, *History of Rome* XXIV, 13-19). The first military operation waged by Marcellus in Sicily was the storming of Leontini. Marcellus utilized his own legions, the 22nd and 23rd that followed him from Campania. It is not clear the reason why Marcellus did not make use of the two *legiones cannenses* in the military operations against Leontini. Livy narrates that the garrison of Leontini was composed by mercenaries

---

26   See A. F. Lazenby, *Hannibal's War, A Military History of the Second Punic War*, Warminster 1978, p. 120. See A. Goldsworthy, *The Fall of Carthage, The Punic Wars 265-146 BC*, London 2003, pp. 260-268 on the war in Sicily.

27   See P. Connolly, *Greece and Rome at War*, London 1981, p. 191. See A.J. Toynbee, *Hannibal's Legacy, The Hannibal War's effects on Roman Life, Rome and her Neighbours after Hannibal's exit*, London 1965, pp. 648-649.

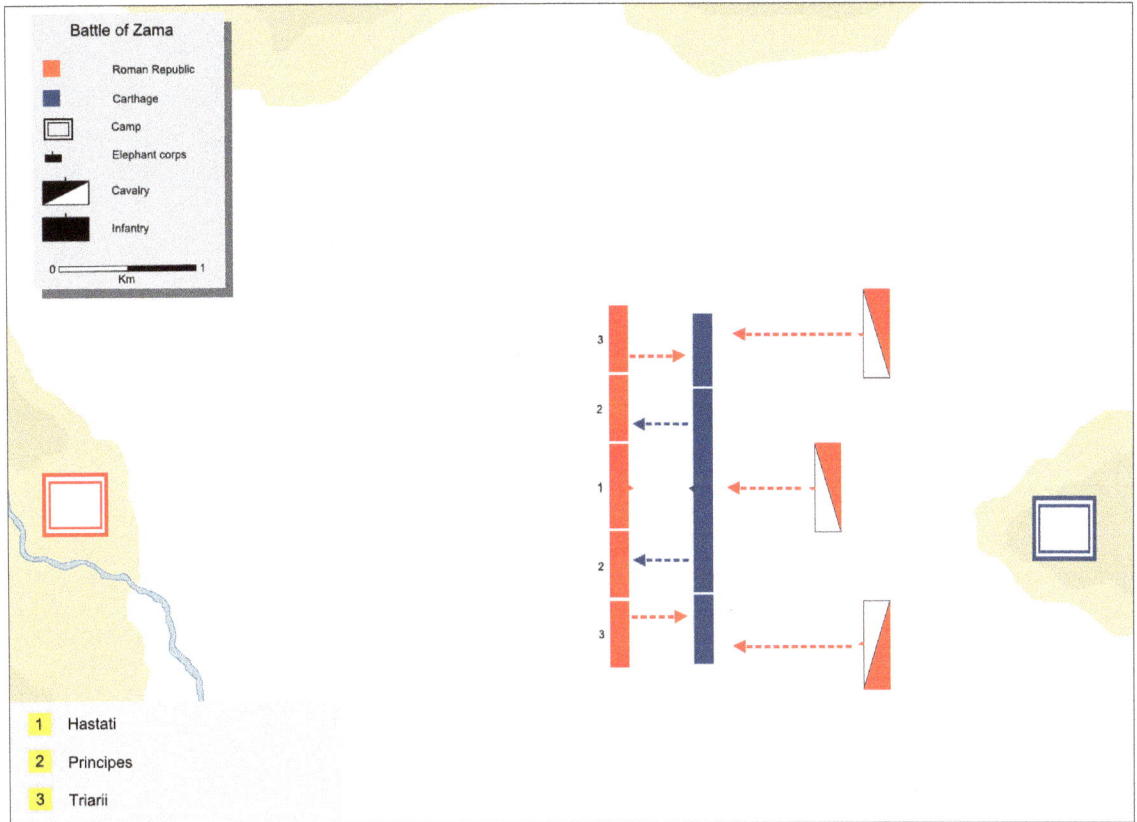

Battle of Zama

- Roman Republic
- Carthage
- Camp
- Elephant corps
- Cavalry
- Infantry

0   1
Km

3
2
1
2
3

1   Hastati
2   Principes
3   Triarii

▲ Battle of Zama, 202 BCE – Scipio and Hannibal reorganize their armies into a single line; the Roman cavalry comes back, attacking Hannibal's infantry from the rear.

and by 2000 Roman deserters (Livy, *History of Rome* XXIV, 30). Marcellus once conquered Leontini, had the deserters flogged and beheaded. Who were these deserters? Did they come from the two *legiones cannenses*? As there were no other Roman soldiers in Sicily at the time, it is the only possibility. Marcellus, thus, at Leontini felt betrayed by the same soldiers that he commanded two years before. Once some of the soldiers coming from the *legiones cannenses* deserted and passed to the Syracusan rebels, the soldiers broke the bond of *fides* between the *patronus* and the *cliens*.

Marcellus, by now *proconsul*, invested Syracuse in the early spring of 213 BCE, supported by the *propraetor* Appius Claudius Pulcher. However Marcellus had to leave the siege of Syracuse to the *proconsul*. The situation deteriorated when a Carthaginians army, commanded by Himilco, joined by Hippocrates occupied Agrigentum (Livy, *History of Rome* XXIV, 35). However, once more, the army collected by Marcellus did not include the two *legiones cannenses*, which were still under the command of the *propraetor* Lentulus.

However, things were going to change. As previously stated, at the beginning of the year 212 BCE, during the consulate of Quintus Fulvius Flaccus and Appius Claudius Pulcher, the soldiers of the *legiones cannenses* appealed to Marcellus (Livy, *History of Rome* XXV, 3). This time, Marcellus called back to active duty the two *legiones cannenses*, when asked by a delegation of soldiers. Livy states that the appeal came from all the soldiers, simple soldiers as well as *centurions* and the cavalrymen. Even the *equites* threw their lot with the infantrymen coming from a less affluent milieu. Marcellus sent the letter to the Senate. The Senate did not change its mind; however, the final decision was left to Marcellus. Marcellus decided to renew his bond or *fides* with the soldiers he once commanded in the wake of Cannae. The situation was once more desperate. As the Carthaginian army of Himilco posed

a new threat, Rome needed all the soldiers available in Sicily. The *legiones cannenses* fought valiantly at the siege of Syracuse (Livy, *History of Rome* XXIX, 1). The years spent under the orders of Marcellus was not in vain. The Roman *consul suffectus* probably detected in the soldiers defeated at Cannae the spirit of the good soldiers. The war in Sicily continued till 210 BCE. However, the two *legiones cannenses*, after the brief parenthesis under Marcellus, did not took part in the military operations. After the end of the hostilities the *legiones cannenses* continued to garrison Sicily till 205 BCE.

Two episodes are recorded in 209 BCE; the first is the amalgamation of the *legiones cannenses* with the survivors of Herdonea and the mass mutiny of the Italic contingent.

The *legiones cannenses* in 209 BCE were reinforced with the survivors of Herdonea (Livy, *History of Rome* XXV, 21-22 and XXVII, 7).[28] This episode is quite important as it makes clear that the *senatus consultum* was still in force and that the *legiones cannenses* were still considered a penal unit. Thus, other soldiers that were thought to have behaved badly were versed in the *legiones cannenses*. In fact, he soldiers of the *legiones cannenses* as well as the survivors of Herdonia were forbidden to camp no less than ten thousand feet near a city.

The situation that looked hopeless this time influenced the behavior of the Italic contingent. Thus, in 209 BCE the Italic contingent mutinied. The soldiers complained that they were in the field already ten years, that they were tired of levies and contributions, and that each year they had to fight and face great defeats (Livy, *History of Rome* XXVII, 9). The consuls immediately sent the mutineers at home, although probably most of the soldiers remained. However, the affair did not end there (Livy, *History of Rome* XXIX, 15). In 204, the incriminated colonies, Nepetes, Sutrii, Ardea, Cales, Sora, Suessa, Setia, Circeii, Narnia and Interamna were punished. Thus the colonies were ordered to enroll a double number of soldiers and 100 cavalrymen for each colony (Livy, *History of Rome* XXIX, 24).[29]

---

28   See also A. F. Lazenby, *Hannibal's War, A Military History of the Second Punic War*, Warminster 1978, p. 174.

29   See A. F. Lazenby, *Hannibal's War, A Military History of the Second Punic War*, Warminster 1978, p. 172.

I - Hastatus and Princeps

The figure on the left, a *hastatus* or *princeps,* wears a red tunic and *caligae*. His head is protected by bronze Montefortino with cheekpieces. He is defended by a *lorica hamata*, which reaches his hips. The shoulder guards, U shaped, are made in linen. He is defended by a *scutum*. He is armed with a heavy *pilum* and with the *gladius hispaniensis*.

The figure on the right, an *hastatus* or *princeps*, wears a red tunic and *caligae* sandals. His head is protected by a bronze Montefortino with cheekpieces. His armor consists in a *cardiopylax*, or *spongia pectoris*, shaped as a muscle cuirass. He is armed with a heavy *pilum*, longer that that of his colleague. His weapons also include the heavy oval shield, or *scutum*, and the long *gladius hispaniensis*. Possibly, in the aftermath of the battle of Cannae, the legionaries adopted whatever weapon or defensive armament was available, albeit continuing in their tasks. Thus, the figure on the left is defended by a cuirass more often seen on *triarii*. The figure on the left, on the other hand, maintained his previous armament, although, possibly the *cardiophylax* had been taken by a rebellious Samnite, slaughtered during a battle.

F. UNDER THE ORDERS OF SCIPIO AFRICANUS (205-202 BCE)

For five more long years Livy does not give us any information. The situation of the *legiones cannenses* changed dramatically at the beginning of 205 BCE, when Publius Cornelius Scipio and Lucius Licinius Crassus were elected consuls (Livy, *History of Rome* XXVIII, 38).

Publius Scipio, the newly elected consul wished to bring the war to Africa. Scipio's new strategy postulated that the only possible way to remove Hannibal and his army from Italy was to attack his own home country, Carthage. Although fiercely opposed by the old Fabius Maximus, who was hostile to the idea of taking away soldiers from Italy, the old *cunctator* was only in part successful in opposing Scipio's plan (Livy, *History of Rome* XXVIII, 40-42). The Senate passed a *senatus consultum* which assigned to Scipio Sicily as province. However, he was given the permission to bring the war to Africa from the territory of his own province. However, the *senatus consultum* did not assign any soldiers to Scipio, but only the permission to bring volunteers.

Scipio had no choice, but to enroll an army of volunteers. Indeed, Livy does not mention any legion levied in the year 205 BCE. Evidently the Roman war effort was exhausted, and probably no more manpower was available. It was obvious to Scipio, once he reached Sicily, that the *legiones cannenses* would constitute the core for the manpower he so desperately needed. Livy reports that Scipio inspected the legions, choosing the soldiers that already fought under Marcellus, because they had a better military discipline, and because they already had experience in besieging cities as Syracuse (Livy, *History of Rome* XXIX, 1).

▲ Various Roman soldiers.

▲ *Golden stater, minted in 196 BCE, depicting on the obverse the head of Titus Quinctius Flamininus, looking right. On the reverse is depicted an inscription, T. Quincti, referring to Titus Quinctius Flamininus, crowned with wreath by Victory standing left.*

Scipio also enrolled in his army not only the same infantrymen, but also the same *equites* who fought at Cannae. As some Sicilian knights were unhappy of military service outside Sicily, Scipio asks from them to give their horse and their weapons to 300 Roman knights, who had already fought various battle and thus they had a high level of experience (Livy, *History of Rome* XXIX, 1). These *equites* were most probably the survivors from the battle of Cannae that the *senatus consultum* had deprived of their state horses as punition, and did length their military service to ten more years with a horse purchased at his expenses.

The remaining volunteers, circa 7000, came from Italic stock. The populations of Umbria as well as the citizens of Nursia, Reates and Amiternum as well as the Sabini, the Marsii, the Peligni, the Marrucini, did enroll as volunteers. The Camertes, which had with the Romans a *foedus aequus* gave a *cohors* of 600 men (Livy, *History of Rome* XXVIII, 45). Also, the war fleet necessary for the expedition to Africa was paid by the allies.

Scipio did every effort to get the two *legiones cannenses*. The two legions were now in fact under the command of the *praetor* M. Pomponius Matho, who received the province of Sicily for the year 204 BCE (Livy, *History of Rome* XXIX, 11). It is possible that the Senate realized that it could have been dangerous to allow to the charismatic Scipio to take to Africa the two *legiones cannenses*. It was clear that after all those years the two units were disaffected to the Senate, but also that these soldiers were willing to obey Cornelius Scipio, who had with them a personal bond. Thus, the Senate probably wished to maintain the two *legiones cannenses* as the garrison of Sicily under the orders of the new governor, the *praetor* M. Pomponius Matho.

However, Scipio wrote to Pomponius Mato asking him which was the limit of soldiers of legionaries and allies that could have been possible to bring to Africa (Livy, *History of Rome* XXIX, 24). The governor of Sicily happily agrees and, thus, Scipio took with him all the *legiones cannenses*. There is a general agreement among scholars that Scipio legions brought to Africa were the *legiones cannenses*.[30] Livy emphasizes in this occasion the personal bond of *fides* between Scipio and the *legiones cannenses*.

---

30   See B. Caven, *The Punic Wars*, London 1980, p. 236. Caven brings the positive opinion of Brunt. See also P. Connolly, *Greece and Rome at War*, London 1981, p. 201 and Toynbee and De Sanctis in A.J. Toynbee, *Hannibal's Legacy, The Hannibal War's effects on Roman Life, Rome and her Neighbours after Hannibal's exit*, London 1965, pp. 648-649.

Thus, Scipio was particularly fond of the soldiers who survived Cannae. Moreover, Scipio was well aware that the soldiers under his command would become in the future his political and social *clientes*, giving him additional influence in the Senate. On the other hand, the soldiers were also fond of Scipio because they knew that he would have had put a term to their shameful military service.

It is quite difficult to reconstruct the total strength of Scipio's army that left Sicily for Africa. Livy reports various and conflicting information on Scipio's total strength (Livy, *History of Rome* XXIX, 25). Thus, according to one source the army formed by Scipio numbered 10.000 infantrymen and 2200 cavalrymen, according to a second source Scipio's army numbered 16.000 infantrymen and 1600 cavalrymen, or according to a third more plausible source Scipio's army numbered 35.000 men. According to Connolly, Scipio's army included 30.000 infantrymen and 6000 cavalrymen. The numbers given by Livy are quite puzzling. The two *legiones cannenses* alone numbered circa 13.000 men and 600 cavalrymen. Thus, the first two sources can only refer only to the *legiones cannenses*, although the high number of cavalrymen is puzzling. Thus, if the third source is corrected, the Italic contingent numbered no less than 21.000 men, of whom at least 3600 were cavalrymen. Still all these numbers can only demonstrate that the two *legiones cannenses* were the backbone of Scipio's army. Only in 204 BCE, after a year, Scipio's army was definitely ready to sail for Africa. Scipio, now *proconsul* concentrated his whole army at Lylibaum. According to Lazenby, Scipio's army consisted in the 7000 Italic volunteers, the *legiones cannenses*, and the remains of the Italic contingent of the *legiones cannenses*.[31]

Scipio landed near Utica, disrupting the plans of the Carthaginians, who were waiting for him at Emporia. Scipio immediately calls for Massinissa, a Numidian prince, who wish to overthrow Syphax, the most important Numidian prince. The latter, married to Sofonisba, the daughter of Hasdrubal, is an important ally of Carthage. However, Massinissa is not just a political pawn in Scipio's attempt to overthrow Carthaginian rule. The Numidian king can also provide the Romans with light cavalry, they so desperately need. After a victorious clash with a contingent of cavalry, Scipio try to conquer the Punic city of Utica, but he fails in the intent and decides to camp for the winter, building the "Castra Cornelia" the fortified camps where he shall winter with all his army. By the spring time of 203 BCE, Scipio feels strong enough to attack the armies of Hasdrubal and Syphax, camped on two adjacent hills. The surprise attack is a success and the enemy's army is annihilated. Hasdrubal retires to Carthage while Syphax returns to Numidia. Thanks to new enlistments and the arrival of 4000 mercenaries from Spain, within a month Hasdrubal and Syphax could resume hostilities, but they are once defeated in the Campi Magni, on the upper course of the Bagrada. Hasdrubal returns to Carthage, while Syphax withdraws to Cirta, the capital of his kingdom. Scipio took advantage of the victory to occupy various cities, from where he can control the enemy's land communications. In the meantime, he sends Laelius and Massinissa in pursuit of Syphax, who is defeated near Cirta and taken prisoner.

---

31   See A. F. Lazenby, *Hannibal's War, A Military History of the Second Punic War*, Warminster 1978, p. 195. See also H.H. Scullard, *Scipio Africanus, Soldier and Politician*, London 1970, pp. 111-115.

J - Triarius and Hastatus or Princeps

The figure on the left, a *triarius*, wears a white tunic and *caligae*. His head is protected by an iron Attic helmet with cheekpieces, with two side feathers. He is covered by a *lorica hamata*, with underneath a *subarmalis* ending in leather *pteryges*. He is defended by a *scutum*. He is armed with his hands he is holding the handle of his sword, a *gladius hispaniensis*.

The figure on the right, an *hastatus* or *princeps*, wears a red tunic and *caligae* sandals. His head is protected by a bronze Montefortino with cheekpieces. His armor consists in a *cardiopylax*, or *spongia pectoris*, shaped as a muscle cuirass. He is armed with a heavy *pilum*. His weapons also include the heavy oval shield, or *scutum*, and the long *gladius hispaniensis*.

1

2

His wife Sofonisbam poisoned herself. Scipio confers t to Massinissa the title of king of Numidia.

By then, Carthage began peace negotiations. The conditions of Scipio were severe. The Roman warlord requested the restitution of prisoners, the withdrawal of the Carthaginian armies from Italy, the formal cession of the Carthaginian territories in Spain, already conquered by the same Scipio in a series of campaigns between 210 and 206 BCE, to the Roman Republic, and the handing of the warships. The Carthaginians, powerless, are forced to accept the Roman conditions (winter 203-202 BCE). However, the Carthaginians take advantage of the truce to call back Hannibal and Mago. Mago dies during the journey back home. Hannibal, however, disembarks with 24.000 men at Leptis Minor. The Carthaginian warlord is able in the help of Tichaeus, a relative of Syphax, who sends him 2000 horsemen. Hannibal also can count on the 12.000 men of Mago, all well-trained soldiers, on new recruits in Africa, and n 4000 Macedonians sent by King Philip.

The devastation of the Bagrada valley, an important source of supply of Carthage, by Scipio, forces Hannibal to meet the Roman warlord, far away from Carthage. Scipio and Hannibal are finally one in front of the others in the plains of Zama.[32] Let's leave once more the description of the battle to our most valued sources, first Polybius, and then Livy.

"XV. 9 1 After this conversation, which held out no hopes of reconciliation, the two generals parted from each other. 2 On the following morning at daybreak they led out their armies and opened the battle, the Carthaginians fighting for their own safety and the dominion of Africa, and the Romans for the empire of the world. 3 Is there anyone who can remain unmoved in reading the narrative of such an encounter? 4 For it would be impossible to find more valiant soldiers, or generals who had been more successful and were more thoroughly exercised in the art of war, nor indeed had Fortune ever offered to contending armies a more splendid prize of victory, since the conquerors would not be masters of Africa and Europe alone, but of all those parts of the world which now hold a place in history; as indeed they very shortly were. 6 Scipio drew up his army in the following fashion. 7 In front he placed the *hastati* with certain intervals between the maniples and behind them the *principes*, not placing their maniples, as is the usual Roman custom, opposite to the intervals separating those of the first line, but directly behind these latter at a certain distance owing to the large number of the enemy's elephants. 8 Last of all he placed the *triarii*. On his left wing he posted Gaius Laelius with the Italian horse, and on the right wing Massanissa with the whole of his Numidians. 9 The intervals of the first maniples he filled up with the cohorts of *velites*, ordering them to open the action, 10 and if they were forced back by the charge of the elephants to retire, those who had time to do so by the straight passages as far as the rear of the whole army, and those who were overtaken to right or left along the intervals between the lines. 10 1 Having made these preparations he rode along the lines and addressed his troops in a few words suitable to the occasion. 2 "Bear in mind," he said, "your past battles and fight like brave men worthy of yourselves and your country. Keep it before your eyes that if you overcome your enemies not only will you be unquestioned masters of Africa, but you will gain for yourselves and your country the undisputed command and sovereignty of the rest of the world. 3 But if the result of the battle be otherwise, those of you who have fallen bravely in the fight will lie for ever shrouded in the glory of dying thus for their country, 4 while those who save themselves by flight will spend the remainder of their lives in misery and disgrace. For no place in Africa will be able to afford you safety, and if you fall into the hands of the Carthaginians it is plain enough to anyone who gives due thought to it what fate awaits you. 5 May none of you, I pray, live to experience that fate. Now that Fortune offers us a choice of the most glorious of prizes, how utterly craven, in short how foolish shall we be, if we reject the greatest of goods and choose the greatest of evils from mere love of life. Go, therefore,

---

32   See A.F. Lazenby, *Hannibal's War, A Military History of the Second Punic War*, Warminster 1978, pp. 193-220. See also A. Goldsworthy, *The Fall of Carthage, The Punic Wars 265-146 BC*, London 2003, pp. 286-300, and G. Brizzi, *Scipione ed Annibale. La guerra per salvare Roma*, Bari 2007, pp. 155-178.

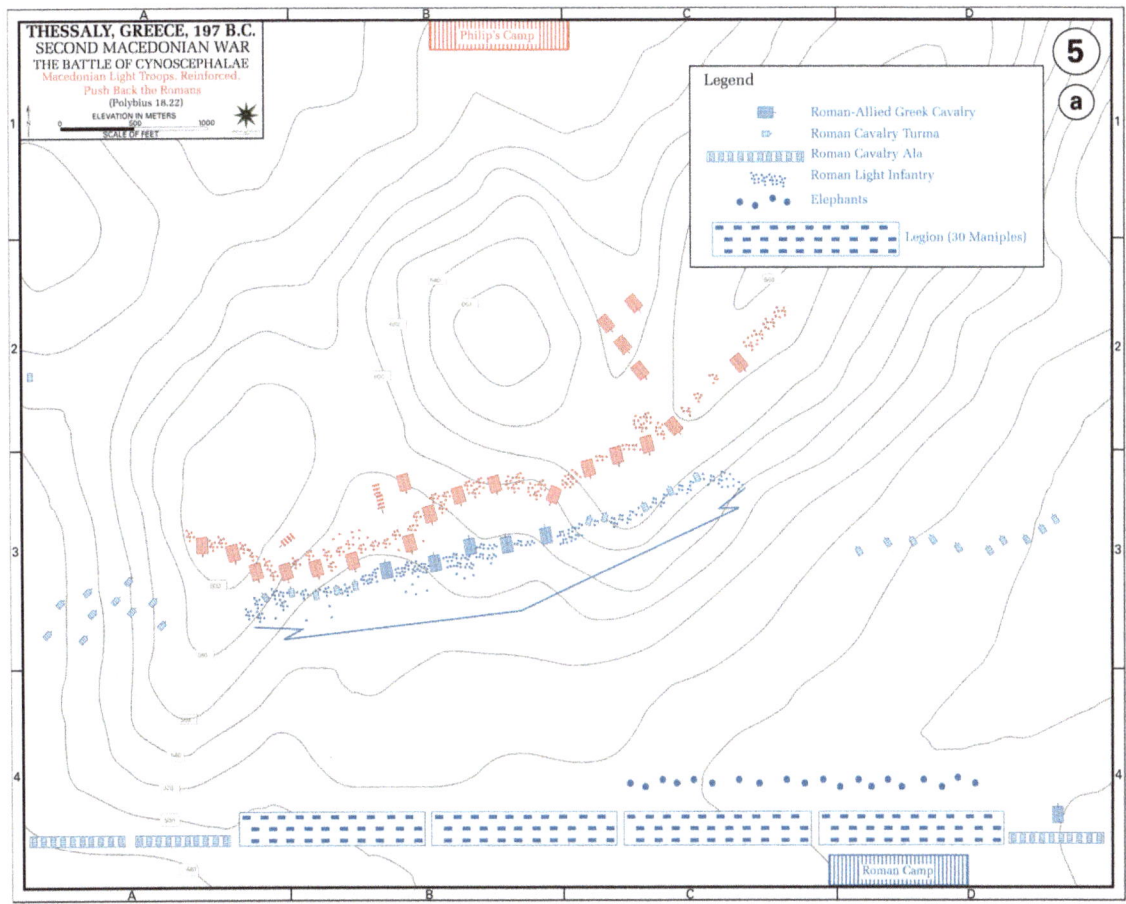

THESSALY, GREECE, 197 B.C.
SECOND MACEDONIAN WAR
THE BATTLE OF CYNOSCEPHALAE
Macedonian Light Troops, Reinforced,
Push Back the Romans
(Polybius 18.22)
ELEVATION IN METERS
SCALE OF FEET

Philip's Camp

5
a

Legend

Roman-Allied Greek Cavalry
Roman Cavalry Turma
Roman Cavalry Ala
Roman Light Infantry
Elephants

Legion (30 Maniples)

Roman Camp

▲ Battle of Cynoscephalae, 197 BCE - Initial Roman and Macedonian armies' deployment.

to meet the foe with two objects before you, emperor victory or death. 7 For men animated by such a spirit must always overcome their adversaries, since they go into battle ready to throw their lives away." 11 1 Such was the substance of Scipio's harangue. Hannibal placed in front of his whole force his elephants, of which he had over eighty, and behind them the mercenaries numbering about twelve thousand. They were composed of Ligurians, Celts, Balearic Islanders, and Moors. 2 Behind these he placed the native Libyans and Carthaginians, and last of all the troops he had brought over from Italy at a distance of more than a stade from the front lines. 3 He secured his wings by cavalry, placing the Numidian allies on the left and the Carthaginian horse on the right. 4 He ordered each commanding officer of the mercenaries to address his own men, bidding them be sure of victory as they could rely on his own presence and that of the forces that he had brought back with him. 5 As for the Carthaginians, he ordered their commanders to set before their eyes all the sufferings that would befall their wives and children if the result of the battle were adverse. They did as they were ordered, 6 and Hannibal himself went the round of his own troops, begging and imploring them to remember their comradeship of seventeen years and the number of the battles they had previously fought against the Romans. 7 "In all these battles," he said, "you proved so invincible that you have not left the Romans the smallest hope of ever being able to defeat you. 8 Above all the rest, and apart from your success in innumerable smaller engagements, keep before your eyes the battle of the Trebia fought against the father of the present Roman general, bear in mind the battle of the Trasimene against Flaminius, and that of Cannae against Aemilius, 9 battles with which the action in which we are about to engage is not worthy of

▲ **Roman Republic Coins minted during the Second Punic War: Quadrigatus:**
Silver, minted in Rome, 225-212 BC; Obverse: Laureate, Janiform head of Dioscuri. Border of dots. Reverse: Jupiter in quadriga, right, driven by Victory. Jupiter holds scepter in left hand and hurls thunderbolt with right hand; incuse on tablet, inscription: ROMA

▲ **Roman Republic Coins minted during the Second Punic War: Semuncia**
Copper alloy, minted in Rome, 217-215 BC Obverse: Head of Mercury, right, wearing winged petasos. Reverse: Prow, right; above, inscription: ROMA

comparison either in respect to the numbers of the forces engaged or the courage of the soldiers." 10 He bade them, as he spoke thus, to cast their eyes on the ranks of the enemy. Not only were they fewer, but they were scarcely a fraction of the forces that had formerly faced them, and for courage they were not to be compared with those. 11 For then their adversaries were men whose strength was unbroken and who had never suffered defeat, but those of to-day were some of them the children of the former and some the wretched remnant of the legions he had so often vanquished and put to flight in Italy. 12 Therefore he urged them not to destroy the glorious record of themselves and their general, but, fighting bravely, to confirm their reputation for invincibility. 13 Such was the substance of the harangues of the two generals. 12 1 When all was ready for battle on both sides, the Numidian horse having been skirmishing with each other for some time, Hannibal ordered the drivers of the elephants to charge the enemy. 2 When the trumpets and bugles sounded shrilly from all sides, some of the animals took fright and at once turned tail and rushed back upon the Numidians who had come up to help the Carthaginians, and Massanissa attacking simultaneously, the Carthaginian left wing was soon left exposed. 3 The rest of the elephants falling on the Roman *velites* in the space between the two main armies, 4 both inflicted and suffered much loss, until finally in their terror some of them escaped through the gaps in the Roman line with Scipio's foresight had provided, so that the Romans suffered no injury, while others fled towards the right and, received by the cavalry with showers of javelins, at length escaped out of the field. 5 It was at this moment that Laelius, availing himself of the disturbance created by the elephants, charged the Carthaginian cavalry 6 and forced them to headlong flight. He pressed the pursuit closely, as likewise did Massanissa. 7 In the meanwhile both phalanxes slowly and in imposing array advanced on each other, except the troops which Hannibal had brought back from Italy, who remained in their original position. 8 When the phalanxes were close to each other, Romans fell upon their foes, raising their war-cry and clashing their shields with their spears as is their practice, 9 while there was a strange confusion of shouts raised by the Carthaginian mercenaries, for, as Homer says, "their voice was not one, but Mixed was the murmur, and confused the sound". Their names all various, as appears from the list of them I gave above. 13 1 As the whole battle was a hand-to-hand affair [the men using neither spears nor swords], the mercenaries at first prevailed by their courage and skill, wounding many of the Romans, 2 but the latter still continued to advance, relying on their admirable order and on the superiority of their arms. 3 The rear ranks of the Romans followed close on their comrades, cheering them on, but the Carthaginians behaved like cowards, never coming near their mercenaries nor attempting to back them up, 4 so that finally the barbarians gave way, and thinking that they had evidently been left in the lurch by their own side, fell upon those they encountered in their retreat and began to kill them. 5 This actually compelled many of the Carthaginians to die like men; for as they were being butchered by their own mercenaries they were obliged against their will to fight both against these and against the Romans, 6 and as when at bay they showed frantic and extraordinary courage, they killed a considerable number both of their mercenaries and of the enemy. 7 In this way they even threw the cohorts of the *hastati* into confusion, but the officers of the *principes*, seeing what was happening, brought up their ranks to assist, 8 and now the greater number of the Carthaginians and their mercenaries were cut to pieces where they stood, either by themselves or by the *hastati*. 9 Hannibal did not allow the survivors in their flight to mix with his own men but, ordering the foremost ranks to level their spears against them, prevented them from being received into his force. 10 They were therefore obliged to retreat towards the wings and the open ground beyond. 14 1 The space which separated the two armies still on the field was now covered with blood, slaughter, and dead bodies, and the Roman general was placed in great difficulty by this obstacle to his completing the rout of the enemy. 2 For he saw that it would be very difficult to pass over the ground without breaking his ranks owing to the quantity of slippery corpses which were still soaked in blood and had fallen in heaps and the number of arms thrown away at haphazard. 3 However, after conveying the wounded to the rear and recalling by bugle those of the *hastati* who were still pursuing the enemy, he stationed the latter in the fore part of the field of battle, opposite the enemy's centre, and making the *principes* and *triarii* close up on both wings ordered them to advance over the dead. 5 When these troops had surmounted the obstacles and found themselves in a line with the *hastati* the two phalanxes closed with the greatest eagerness and ardour. 6 As they were nearly equal in numbers as well as in spirit and bravery, and were equally well armed, the contest was for long doubtful, the men falling where they stood out of determination, 7 and Massanissa and Laelius, returning from the pursuit of the cavalry, arrived providentially at the proper moment. 8 When they fell on Hannibal's army from the rear, most of the men were cut down in their ranks, while of those who took to flight only quite a few escaped, as the cavalry were close on them and the country was level. 9 More than fifteen hundred Romans fell, the Carthaginian loss amounting to twenty thousand killed and nearly the same number of prisoners."[33]

"XXX.32. Arrived at their camps, they both ordered their soldiers to have arms and their spirits in readiness for the final conflict to make them victors, if success attended them, not for one day but forever. [2] Whether Rome or Carthage should give laws to the nations they would know the next day before nightfall. For not Africa, they said, or Italy but the whole world would be the reward of victory —a reward matched by the danger for those whom the fortune of battle should not favour. [3] In fact the Romans had no way of escape open in a foreign and an unknown land, and for Carthage, once it had poured out its last resources, immediate destruction seemed impending.[4] For this decision on the following day two generals far and away the most distinguished and two of the bravest armies of the two wealthiest nations went forth, on that day either to crown the many distinctions heretofore won, or to bring them to naught. [5] Consequently a wavering between hope and fear confused their spirits; and as they surveyed now their own battle-line, now that of the enemy, while weighing their strength more by the eye than by calculation, the bright side and at the same time the dark was before their minds. What did not occur to the men themselves of their own accord the generals would suggest in admonition and exhortation. [6] The Carthaginian kept recalling to their minds the achievements of sixteen years in the land of Italy, so many Roman generals, so many armies wiped out completely, and brave deeds of individuals, whenever he came to a soldier distinguished in the record of some battle. [7] Scipio would recall the Spanish provinces and recent battles in Africa and the enemy's admission, in that on account of fear they could but sue for peace, and yet had been unable to abide by

---

33   Polybius IV, *Histories*, Books 9-15 (Translation of William R. Paton; Loeb Classical Library; Cambridge, Harvard University Press 1922).

K - *Triarius* and *Hastatus*, or *Princeps*

The figure on the left, a *triarius*, wears a red tunic and *perones*, or high boots. His head is protected by bronze Attic helmet with cheekpieces, with two side feathers. He is covered by a long *lorica hamata*, which reaches his hips. He is defended by a *scutum*. He is armed with a *gladius hispaniensis* and a spear.

The figure on the right, an *hastatus* or *princeps*, wears a red tunic and *caligae*, or sandals. His head is protected by a bronze Montefortino with cheekpieces. His armor consists in a long *lorica hamata*, which reaches his hips. He is armed with a heavy *pilum*. His weapons also include the heavy oval shield, or *scutum*, and the long *gladius hispaniensis*.

The *triarius* and the *hastatus* or *princeps* by now, after many years of fighting, look alike in their appearance. The only difference in their armament is that the *triarius* is armed with a spear and the *hastatus* or *princeps* with the heavy *pilum*. These two tired legionaries are getting ready for an inspection, possibly before the battle of Zama. By now, organized in *cohortes*, and not in *manipula*, the Roman heavy infantryman looks like the mules of Marius, the legionaries who won Gaul for Julius Caesar.

1

2

the peace on account of their ingrained perfidy. [8] Furthermore, as his conference with Hannibal had been in private and could be freely altered, he gave it the direction he desired. [9] He divined that as the Carthaginians went out into battle-line, the gods had given them the same omens as when their fathers fought at the Aegates Islands. [10] The end of the war and hardship was at hand, he said, the spoils of Carthage within reach, and the return home to their native city, to parents, children, wives and household gods. So erect did he stand as he spoke these words, and with so happy a look on his face that one would have believed him already the victor. 33. However, he did not form cohorts1 in close contact, each in advance of its standards, but rather maniples at a considerable distance from each other, so that there should be an interval where the enemy's elephants might be driven through without breaking up the ranks. [2] Laelius, whom he had previously had in his service as lieutenant, but in the present year as quaestor, assigned not by lot but by decree of the senate, was posted with the Italic cavalry on the left wing, Masinissa and the Numidians on the right. [3] The open passages between the maniples of the front line troops Scipio filled with *velites*, the light-armed of that day, under orders that, upon the charge of the elephants, they should either flee behind the ranks in the line, or else dashing to right and left and closing up to the maniles in the van, should give the beasts an opening through which they might rush among missiles hurled from both sides.[4] Hannibal in order to create a panic drew up his elephants in front, and there were eighty of them, a number he had never before had in any battle. [5] Next in order he placed the Ligurian and Gallic auxiliaries in combination with Balearic and Mauretanian troops; in the second line Carthaginians and Africans and the legion of Macedonians. [6] Then, leaving a moderate interval, he drew up a reserve line of Italic soldiers, most of these Bruttians, more of whom [7] had followed him under compulsion and of necessity than of their own consent as he retired from Italy. [8] As for the cavalry, he also placed them on the wings; the Carthaginians held the right wing, the Numidians the left. In an army made up of so many men who had no language, no custom, no law, no arms, no clothing and general appearance in common, nor the same reason for serving, exhortation took various forms. [9] To the auxiliaries was offered pay in cash and greatly increased by a share in the booty. The Gauls had their own inbred hatred of the Romans fanned into flame. [10] Ligurians were offered as an incentive to victory the rich plains of Italy, once they were brought down from their rugged mountains. [11] Mauretanians and Numidians were frightened by Hannibal with the prospect of Masinissa's tyrannical rule. To different nations different hopes and fears were displayed. The Carthaginians' attention was called to the walls of their city, to household gods, tombs of ancestors, children and parents and terror-stricken wives, to destruction and servitude on the one hand, on the other to rule over the world, to the absence of any ground between the extremes of fear and hope.[12] Just as the general was thus speaking among the Carthaginians, and the national leaders among their countrymen, mainly through interpreters, since foreigners were intermingled, trumpets [13] and horns sounded on the Roman side, and such shouts were8 raised that the elephants turned against their own men, especially against the left wing, the Mauretanians and Numidians. Masinissa easily increased their panic and stripped that end of the line of its cavalry support. [14] A few of the beasts, however, being fearlessly driven into the enemy, caused great losses among the ranks of the light-armed, though suffering many wounds themselves. [15] For springing back to the maniples the light-armed made way for the elephants, to avoid being trampled down, and then would hurl their lances from both sides against the beasts doubly exposed to missiles. Nor was there any slackening in the javelins of the men in the front lines until these elephants also, driven out of the Roman line and into their own men by missiles showered upon them from all sides, put the right wing, even the Carthaginian cavalry, to flight. [16] Laelius, on seeing the enemy in confusion, increased their panic. 34. On both sides the Punic battle-line had been stripped of its cavalry when the infantry clashed, now no longer matched either in their hopes or in their strength. In addition there were what seem small things to mention, but at the same time were highly important in the battle: a harmony in

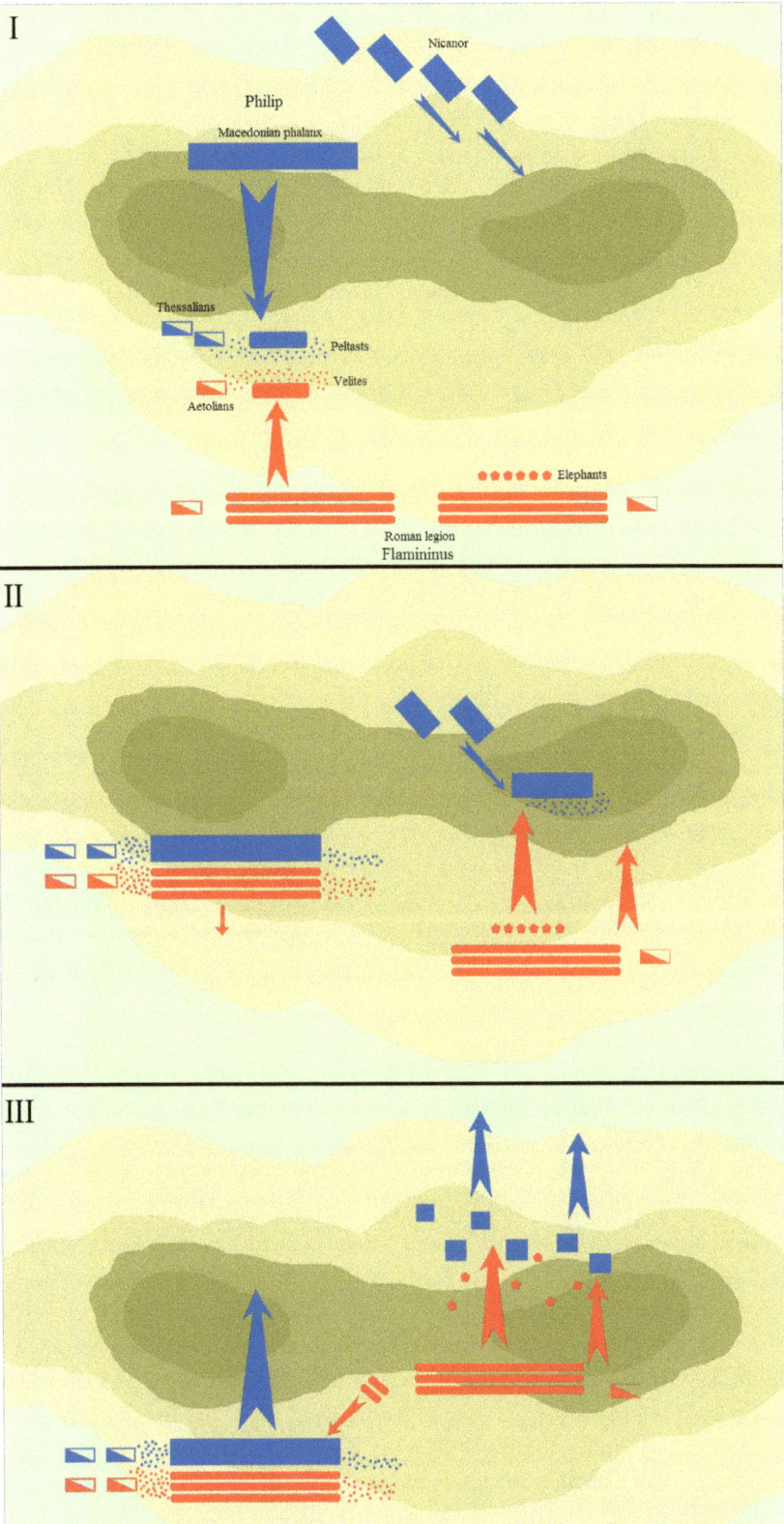

▲ Battle of Cynoscephalae, 197 BCE – I: Philip V initial's attack; II: The Macedonian right wing defeats the Roman left wing; the Roman right wing breaks though the Macedonian left wing; III: The Roman final onslaught.

the shouting of the Romans, which consequently was greater in volume and more terrifying; [2] on the other side discordant voices, as was natural from many nations with a confusion of tongues; for the Romans a battle of little movement, as they pressed on into the enemy by their own weight and that of their arms; on the other side repeated charges at high speed but with less power. [3] Consequently by the first attack the Romans at once dislodged the enemy's line. [4] Then beating them back with their shoulders and the bosses of their shields, being now in close contact with men forced from their position, they made considerable progress, as no one offered any resistance, while as soon as they saw that the enemy's line had given way, even the rear line pressed upon the first, a circumstance which of itself gave them great force in repulsing the enemy. [5] Among the enemy so far was their second line, the Africans and Carthaginians, from supporting the auxiliaries as they gave way, that on the contrary they even drew back for fear the enemy, by slaying the men of the first line if these stoutly resisted, should reach themselves. [6] Accordingly the auxiliaries suddenly retreated and facing their own men, some found refuge in the second line, others, having been refused aid shortly before, and also admission now to the ranks, slashed at those who would not make place for them. [7] And by this time there were almost two battles in one, since the Carthaginians were forced to engage with the enemy and at the same time with their own men. [8] Nevertheless even so they did not admit the panic-stricken, angry men into the line, but closing up their ranks, they forced them out upon the wings and into the empty plain on this side and that outside of the battle, in order not to contaminate their own line, still intact and fresh, with soldiers alarmed by the flight and their wounds. [9] But such heaps of bodies and arms had covered the place where the auxiliaries had stood shortly before that to make their way across was almost more difficult than it had been through the dense mass of the enemy. [10] Accordingly the men of the front line, the *hastati*, pursuing the enemy wherever they could over heaps of bodies and arms and through pools of blood, broke up both their own maniples and their ranks. [11] The maniples of the *principes* also began to waver, as they saw the unsteady line in front of them. When Scipio saw this, he ordered the recall to be sounded at once for the *hastati*, and after withdrawing the wounded to the rear line, he led the *principes* and *triarii* to the wings, in order that the centre, composed of *hastati*, might be safer and steadier. [12] Thus began an entirely new battle. For they had reached the real enemy, their equals in the character of their weapons and their experience in war and the celebrity of their deeds and the greatness whether of their hopes or of [13] their danger. But the Roman was superior both in numbers and in spirit, because he had already routed the cavalry, had already routed the elephants, and was already fighting against the second line, having repulsed the first. 35. At the right moment Laelius and Masinissa, who had pursued the routed cavalry for a considerable distance, returned and dashed into the rear of the enemy's line. That charge of the cavalry finally worsted the enemy. [2] Many were overpowered and slain in the battle-line, many were scattered in flight over the open plain all around, and as the cavalry were in complete possession, they perished everywhere. Over twenty thousand of the Carthaginians and their allies were slain on that day. [3] About the same number were captured, together with one hundred and thirty-two military standards and eleven elephants. Of the victors about fifteen hundred fell. [4] Hannibal, escaping with a few horsemen in the midst of the confusion, fled to Hadrumetum, having tried every expedient both before the battle and during the engagement before he withdrew from the fray. [5] And even by Scipio's admission and that of all the military experts he had achieved this distinction, that he had drawn up his line that day with extraordinary skill: [6] the elephants in the very front, that their haphazard charge and irresistible strength might prevent the Romans from following their standards and keeping their ranks, upon which tactics they based most of their hopes; [7] then the auxiliaries in front of the line of Carthaginians, that men who were brought together from the offscouring of all nations and held not by loyalty but by their pay might have no way of escape open to them; [8] that at the same time, as they met the first fiery attack of the enemy, they might exhaust them, and if they could do no more, might blunt the

▲ **Coins minted by Hannibal during the Second Punic War** – *Shekel*
Silver, minted in Spain, at Carthago Nova, 221-206 BC Obverse: Laureate male head (Melqart or Hannibal) facing left, club over right shoulder; Reverse: Elephant standing right. Repair work evident on the elephant's body.

▲ **Coins minted by Hannibal during the Second Punic War** – Half-Shekel
Minted in Bruttium, 216-209 BC Obverse: Wreathed head of Tanit, with earrings and necklace. Reverse: Horse standing and looking to right; in the background a palm – tree.

enemy's swords by their own wounds; [9] next in order the soldiers in whom lay all his hopes, the Carthaginians and Africans, that being equal to the Romans in everything else, they might have the advantage in fighting with strength undiminished against the weary and the wounded; then, removed to the last line and separated by an open space as well, the Italic troops, of whom it was uncertain whether they were allies or enemies. [10] Having produced this as his last masterpiece Hannibal after his flight to Hadrumetum was called away, returning to Carthage in the thirty-sixth year after he had left it as a boy. [11] Thereupon in the Senate House he admitted that he had been defeated not only in a battle but also in the war, and that there was no hope of safety except in successfully suing for peace."[34]

---

34   Livy VIII, *The History of Rome, Books 28-30* (Translation of Frank G. Moore; Loeb Classical Library; Cambridge, Harvard University Press 1949).

▲ **Coins minted by Hannibal during the Second Punic War** – 1/5 Shekel
Æ, minted in Spain, at Carthago Nova, 221-218 BC Obverse: Wreathed head of Tanit. Reverse: Crested Thracian helmet.

In 200 BCE, once Hannibal had been definitely defeated and Carthage begged for peace, the Roman Republic was free to move once more against Philip V of Macedonia. Rome and Macedonia had already fought a war over Illyria, the First Macedonian War, which ended in a stalemate. This time, two eastern powers, Pergamum and Rhodes appealed to Rome against the expansionistic ambitions of Philip V. After an initial hesitation, also the Aetolian League joined the Roman Republic.

In the wake of the battle of Zama, the *legions cannenses*, as the rest of the Roman army was demobilized. In the year 203 BCE there were still twenty legions under arms. In the year 202 BCE, after Hannibal left Italy there were only sixteen legions, and in the year 201 BCE there were fifteen legions. Brizzi, emphasizes that even before the African campaign, Scipio did his best to send home the oldest of the veterans stemming from the *legiones cannenses*. These could have been people, who were under his command already in 218 BCE.[35]

As, I wrote before, Scipio took care of the soldiers and distributed to his veterans of the *legions cannenses* land allotments in Apulia and Samnium, made available by the Senate.

However, some of the veterans stemming from the *legiones cannenses* did not reached so fast to their new land allotments. In 200 BCE, when the Second Macedonian War began, the army of Africa was probably still not completely demobilized. The consul Sulpicius Galba was given permission to enlist volunteers from Scipio's African army (Livy, *History of Rome* XXXI, 8.). The Senate made a provision that no volunteer was to be enrolled against his will. Probably, around 5000 volunteers from the *legiones cannenses* answered to the Rome's call to arms and fought in the Second Macedonian War. Thus, Livy narrates that 2000 soldiers from Scipio's Africa army mutinied to the consul Publius Villius Tappulus at the beginning of the year 199 BCE (Livy, *History of Rome* XXXII, 3). Later on, Livy reports that Quictius Flamininus enrolled in the year 198 BCE, as supplement to the legions, 3000 infantrymen and 300 cavalry (Livy, *History of Rome* XXXII, 8-9). Slightly later Livy states that Flamininus selected soldiers who served in Spain or Africa, thus veterans of Scipio. A good part of these 3300 soldiers were probably veterans from the *legiones cannenses*.

It is probable that the *senatus consultum* that called for volunteers from Scipio's army was in part devised by Scipio himself. However, Will argues that it was dire necessity that brought P. Sulpicius Galba to constitute his legions with African veterans. By the end of the Second Punic War manpower was lacking and recruitment was growing difficult. On the other hand, Roman veterans did not wish to come home to devastated lands. As result, in the year 200 BCE, only six legions were in arms against Macedonia. Moreover, Scipio Africanus was perceived as one of those responsible for the Second Macedonian War. Thus because of necessity, and because they were called indirectly to serve their *patronus*, part of the veterans from the Cannae legions came to serve the army of the consul Sulpicius Galba. Indeed, as previously stated, some of the decemviri, appointed in 201 BCE to assign land to Scipio African's veterans were probably close collaborators of the Africanus, and two of them commanded the same veterans in the Macedonian campaign, Publius Villius Tappulus and T. Quintius Flamininus. Tappulus and Flamininus played an important part in the last years of the *legiones cannenses*, as the last of the warlords who commanded the *legiones cannenses*, after Marcellus and Scipio.[36]

Less than a year after they arrived in Macedonia, the first 2000 Cannae veterans mutinied (Livy, *History of Rome* XXXII, 3). The soldiers complained that they did not give their consent to further military

---

35   See A.J. Toynbee, *Hannibal's Legacy, The Hannibal War's effects on Roman Life, Rome and her Neighbours after Hannibal's exit*, London 1965p. 647. The data presented by Appian and Livy is accepted by De Sanctis and Toynbee. See G. Brizzi, *Scipione ed Annibale. La guerra per salvare Roma*, Bari 2007, p. 151.

36   See E. Will, *Histoire politique du monde hellénistique, 323-30 av. J.-C.*, Paris 2003, pp. 142 and 148-149. See F., Cassola, *I gruppi politici romani nel III secolo a. C.*, Roma 1962.

service and that they had been embarked by the *tribuni militum* against their will. Besides, they had served enough years in Sicily and Africa. The consul replied that their demand for discharge deemed to be right, and he promised to write to the Senate. Sulpicius Galba, their commander, probably not associated to Scipio and his political group, was not very empathetic to the veterans. The consul Sulpicius Galba did not respect the provision of the *senatus consultum* that no veteran could be enrolled against his will and probably misbehaved towards the soldiers. However, his colleague, the consul Publius Villius Tappulus, once faced with a mutiny immediately capitulated. Tappulus was associated to Scipio, as he was of the *decemviri* selected in 201 BCE. He was well aware that their *patronus* has great influence in Rome. The mutiny itself is also very important. As the Cannae veterans feel discontented, they do mutiny. This behavior is atypical in the army of the middle Republic made of citizen soldiers, but it is typical of the professional army of the late Republic from Marius onwards. Once the soldiers are unhappy, or feel "betrayed" by their leaders, they mutiny.

In the year 198 BCE, Flaminius brought to Greece 3000 more veterans of Scipio's campaigns in Spain and in Africa (Livy, *History of Rome* XXXIII, 8-9). This time the veterans did not mutiny. Besides, the

---

L – Hannibal's Army (1) – The African Core

On the left, a Punic officer, a *Rav Mahanat*, on the right, a Lybio-Phoenician infantryman, and, in the background a Numidian light cavalryman. Polybius says that the core of the Carthaginian army consisted in half caste Lybio-Phoenicians. Barracks built in the wall of Carthage suggest the possibility that its standing army amounted to 20.000 infantrymen and 4000 cavalrymen.

The *Rav Mahanat*, wears a red tunic and closed sandals. He is defended by an Attic- Thracian helmet, a white *linothorax*, ending with two rows of *pteryges*, and an *aspis*, the round hoplitic shield, albeit with slightly reduced dimensions, decorated with Tanit and an inversed crescent. He is armed with a *kopis*, a single edged slashing sword with a curved blade. His helmet is depicted on a coin, minted by the Barcids, while his armor is represented on the reliefs of the Chemtou Mausoleum, from Numidia.

The Lybio-Phoenician infantryman, possibly a veteran at Zama, wears a long red tunic and pointed eastern shoes. His head is protected by a *pilos* conical helmet. His body defense consists in a trilobite cuirass. His shield is probably a Roman scutum, or, possibly a Celtic shield, decorated in the upper part with a palmetto behind a horse. He grips a Greek type of *xiphos*. The trilobite cuirass was associated to Samintes, Bruttii, and Campanians. Possibly it was looted during the Italian campaign. However, a trilobite cuirass found in Ksour es-Saaf cemetery points to the possibility that this type of cuirass was also produced locally. Similar defensive armament is depicted on the stele of Bodmilqart son of Sthenius, son of Accius, son of Pakis, possibly a Carthaginian of Italic origin.

Numidian cavalryman came from Numidia, today Algeria. The region was divided by petty chiefs, often at war with one another, but, all the same, vassals of Carthage. Cavalry was the backbone of their armies, used for razzias. The main characteristic of the Numidian horsemen is that they rode bare back, and that no bridle nor bit were used. Numidian horsemen made a wonderful light cavalry. Useless as shock troops, as they lacked heavy equipment, they were, however, very useful in skirmish or in the pursuit of a fleeing enemy. Dashing toward the enemy, they would throw at him the javelins and retreat, as fast as they came. They never offered contact. The only depiction of these light infantrymen comes from the reliefs on Trajan's column, which depicts the cavalrymen, dressed in a short tunic, armed with a round shield, and two javelins. While at the beginning of the Second Punic War, Hannibal's Army was armed with a typical Hellenistic weaponry, in the wake of Hannibal's early victories in Italy, for example at the Trasimeno, the Punic soldiers adopted Roman weaponry taken from the fallen enemy, such as large quantities of *loricae hamatae*. Yet Hannibal was a good strategist, but a mediocre tactic. Thus, till the end, the heavy infantry continued to fight as the rigid Macedonian phalanx, succumbing under the more mobile Roman infantry.

political connections between Flamininus and Scipio were very close.[37] Flamininus fully appreciated the military potential of the Cannae's veterans. In the spring of 197 BCE, Flamininus finally succeeded in bringing Philip V of Macedonia to battle.

Thus, at Cynoscephalae the Macedonian phalanx was defeated by an army which included Cannae's veterans. Flamininus army included 18.000 Romans and Italics as well as 8000 Greeks, mostly Aetolians. The Cannae's veterans, around 5000 men, were thus around a third of Flamininus army. Let's leave for one last time the description of the battle to our most valued sources, first Polybius, and then Livy.

"XVIII 18 1 Flamininus, not being able to discover where the enemy were encamped, but knowing for a certainty that they were in Thessaly, ordered all his soldiers to cut stakes for a palisade to carry with them for use when required. 2 This appears to be impossible when the Greek usage is followed, but on the Roman system it is easy to cut them. 3 For the Greeks have difficulty in holding only their pikes when on the march and in supporting the fatigue caused by their weight, 4 but the Romans, hanging their long shields from their shoulders by leather straps and only holding their javelins in their hands, can manage to carry the stakes besides. 5 Also the stakes are quite different. 6 For the Greeks consider that stake the best which has the most and the stoutest offshoots all round the main stem, 7 while the stakes of the Romans have but two or three, or at the most four strange lateral prongs, and these all on one side and not alternating. 8 The result of this is that they are quite easy to carry — for one man can carry three or four, making a bundle of them, and when put to use they are much more secure. 9 For the Greek stakes, when planted round the camp, are in the first place easily pulled up; since when the portion of a stake that holds fast closely pressed by the earth is only one, and the offshoots from it are many and large, and when two or three men catch hold of the same stake by its lateral branches, it is easily pulled up 11 Upon this an entrance is at once created owing to its size, and the ones next to it are loosened, because in such a palisade the stakes are intertwined and criss-crossed in few places. 12 With the Romans it is the reverse; for in planting them they so intertwine them that it is not easy to see to which of the branches, the lower ends of which are driven into the ground, the lateral prongs belong, nor to which prongs the branches belong. 13 So, as these prongs are close together and adhere to each other, and as their points are carefully sharpened, it is not easy to pass one's hand through and grasp the stake, nor if one does get hold of it, is it easy to pull it up, as in the first place the power of resistance derived from the earth by all the portions open to attack is almost absolute, and next because a man who pulls at one prong is obliged to lift up numerous other stakes which give simultaneously under the strain owing to the way they are intertwined, and it is not at all probable that two or three men will get hold of the same stake. 16 But if by main force a man succeeds in pulling up one or two, the gap is scarcely observable. 17 Therefore, as the advantages of this kind of palisade are very great, the stakes being easy to find and easy to carry and the whole being more secure and more durable when constructed, 18 it is evident that if any Roman military contrivance is worthy of our imitation and adoption this one certainly is, in my own humble opinion at least. 19 1 To resume — Flamininus, having prepared these stakes to be used when required, advanced slowly with his whole force and established his camp at a distance of about fifty stades from Pherae. 2 Next day at daybreak he sent out scouts to see if by observation and inquiry they could find any means of discovering where the enemy were and what they were about. 3 Philip, at nearly the same time, on hearing that the Romans were encamped near Thebes, left Larisa with his entire army and advanced marching in the direction of Pherae. 4 When at a distance of thirty stades from that town he encamped there while it was still early and ordered all his men to occupy themselves with the care of their persons. 5 Next day at early dawn he aroused his men, and sending on in advance those accustomed to precede the main body with orders

37   See also H.H. Scullard, *Scipio Africanus, Soldier and Politician*, London 1970, pp. 181-182. On Flamininus and Scipio see E. Will, *Histoire politique du monde hellénistique, 323-30 av. J.-C.*, Paris 2003, p. 154. See also E. Badian, "The family and early career of T. Quinctius Flamininus", *Journal of Roman Studies* 61, 1971, pp. 102-111, J. Briscoe, "Flamininus and Roman Politics, 200-189 B. C.", *Latomus* 31, 1972, pp. 22-53.

▲ Various Carthaginian soldiers.

to cross the ridge above Pherae, he himself, when day began to break, moved the rest of his forces out of the camp. 6 The advanced sections of both armies very nearly came into contact at the pass over the hills; 7 for when in the early dusk they caught sight of each other, they halted when already quite close and sent at once to inform their respective commanders of the fact and inquire what they should do. 8 It was decided to remain for that day in their actual camp and to recall the advanced forces. 9 Next day both commanders sent out some horse and light-armed infantry — about three hundred of either arm to reconnoitre. Among these Flamininus included two squadrons of Aetolians owing to their acquaintance with the country. 10 The respective forces met on the near side of Pherae, in the direction of Larisa, and a desperate struggle ensued. 11 As the force under Eupolemus the Aetolian fought with great vigour and called up the Italians to take part in the action, the Macedonians found themselves hard pressed. 12 For the present, after prolonged skirmishing, both forces separated and retired to their camps. 20 1 Next day both armies, dissatisfied with the ground near Pherae, as it was all under cultivation and covered with walls and small gardens, retired from it. 2 Philip for his part began to march towards Scotussa, hoping to procure supplies from that town and afterwards when fully furnished to find ground suitable for his own army. 3 But Flamininus, suspecting his purpose, put his army in motion at the same time as Philip with the object of destroying the corn in the territory of Scotussa before his adversary could get there. 4 As there were high hills between the two armies in their march neither did the Romans perceive where the Macedonians were marching to nor the Macedonians the Romans. 5 After marching all that day, Flamininus having reached the place called Eretria in Phthiotis and Philip the river Onchestus, they both encamped at those spots, each ignorant of the position of the other's camp. 6 Next day they again advanced and encamped, Philip at the place called Melambium in the territory of Scotussa and Flamininus at the sanctuary of Thetis in that of Pharsalus, being still in ignorance of each others' whereabouts. 7 In the night there was a violent thunderstorm accompanied by rain, and next morning at early dawn all the mist from the clouds descended on the earth, so that

1

2

owing to the darkness that prevailed one could not see even people who were close at hand. 8 Philip, however, who was in a hurry to effect his purpose, broke up his camp and advanced with his whole army, but finding it difficult to march owing to the mist, after having made but little progress, he intrenched his army and sent off his covering force with orders to occupy the summits of the hills which lay between him and the enemy. 21 1 Flamininus lay still encamped near the sanctuary of Thetis and, being in doubt as to where the enemy were, he pushed forward ten squadrons of horse and about a thousand light-armed infantry, sending them out with orders to go over the ground reconnoitring cautiously. 2 In proceeding towards the pass over the hills they encountered the Macedonian covering

---

M – Hannibal's Army (2) – Celtic and Iberian Mercenaries

Most of Hannibal armies consisted in treacherous and unreliable Celt and Iberian mercenaries. Contrary to the trustworthy Africans, these mercenaries could not cope with discipline and often fought as an unorganized rabble, albeit, from time to time with the well know "furia gallica".

The figure on the left depicts a Celtic chieftain. He wears a long white tunic, bordered in red, *bracae*, or trousers, for the Roman a symbol of effeminacy, and a wooden mantle, with a texture quite similar to that of the Scottish tartan. His head is covered by the Celtic variation of the Montefortino helmet, here made in bronze. Its main characteristic is the triple-disc cheek pieces. These helmets could present a round cap, or, as in the illustration, a top knot. However, helmets were expensive. Most warriors, as narrated by Diodorus, would simply wash their hair with lime, combing it to looks like a horse mane. The only body armor of our warrior is a simple breastplate and round plate as well as a heavy belt. Richer and more powerful chief would had sported a *lorica hamata*, characterized by a cape that hangs over the shoulders. The oval flat shield was made in oak planks. Quite flat, in fact it was slightly tapered toward the sides. As the Roman *scutum*, it had a wooden spindle shaped boss. At the beginning rectangular, the shape of the boss evolved to that of a butterfly. The center of the boss, hallowed, permitted to grasp the handle. These shields were covered with hide. Three wooden shields had been discovered at La Tène. He is armed with a spear, which could reach the length of 2.5 m, and a long sword. The Celtic sword evolved in three distinctive periods, the Early Period (450 – 250 BCE), the Middle Period (250-120 BCE), and the Late period (120-50 BCE). In the period considered, the Middle Period, sword's blades were increasing in length, reaching 75-80 cm. Besides, they were round ended. Together with swords, also metal sheaths had been found. Their main characteristic was a prominent chape. The traditional handle had the shape of an elongated X. Celts, could fight in small companies, marshalling around a standard. These were figurine set on a pole, shaped as animals, for example, wild boars. The use of standards is attested in the reliefs on the arch from Orange. Signals were given with a *carnyx*, a long trumpet shaped instrument, with a mouth fashioned as an animal head. Horn blowers and standard bearers are, on the other hand, depicted on relief from Bormio. Still, the main weakness of the Celts was that warriors were very individualistic. However, at least till the battle of Telamone, Celtic warriors like to defy their enemy at individual duels, fighting naked to emphasize their prowess. Our warrior does not display the torques, the twisted neck ring, which had become one of the main characteristics of the Celtic warrior.

The figure on the right is an Iberian horseman. No less than 8000 of the 20.000 soldiers, who reached Italy, were Iberians. He wears a white tunic, bordered in red, and shoes. His head is covered by a helmet. He is defended by a small round shield, which he carries on his back. He is armed with a long heavy spear and a falcata sword. Indeed, Polybius states that Iberians were dressed in short white tunics bordered with crimson. Bronze helmets as shown in the picture were rare. Most of the Iberians wore a crested head gear, probably made of sinew, which is described by Strabo. Infantrymen had large oval shield of the Celtic type. However, cavalrymen had a small round shield with a central hand grip, as the one shown in the figure. The main weapon was the falcata, a sword used to cut and thrust, quite similar to the Greek *kopis*. A short knife was fastened to the sword's scabbard. Many figurines depict a broad belt, probably in leather, which was used to hold the scabbard. While this cavalryman has a spear, javelins similar to the *pilum* were used by the infantry. Besides, the *saunion*, a barbed javelin entirely of iron, was also used. Iberian infantry included slingers, from the Baleares, as well as heavy infantry, sometimes defended by mail armor. Cavalry often reached the battlefield riding, but then, dismounted to fight. A girth strap holds in place the bridle and the saddle blanket.

force quite unexpectedly owing to the obscurity of the army. 3 Both forces were thrown somewhat into disorder for a short time but soon began to take the offensive, sending to their respective commanders messengers to inform them of what had happened. 4 When in the combat that ensued the Romans began to be overpowered and to suffer loss at the hands of the Macedonian covering force they sent to their camp begging for help, 5 and Flamininus, calling upon Archedamus and Eupolemus the Aetolians and two of his military tribunes, 6 sent them off with five hundred horse and two thousand foot. 7 For the Romans, encouraged by the arrival of the reinforcements, fought with redoubled vigour, 8 and the Macedonians, though defending themselves gallantly, were in their turn pressed hard, and upon being completely overmastered, fled to the summits and sent to the king for help. 22 1 Philip, who had never expected, for the reasons I have stated, that a general engagement would take place on that day, had even sent out a fair number of men from his camp to forage, 2 and now when he heard of the turn affairs were taking from the messengers, and as the mist was beginning to clear, he called upon Heraclides of Gyrton, the commander of the Thessalian horse, and Leo, who was in command of the Macedonian horse, and dispatched them, together with all the mercenaries except those from Thrace, under the command of Athenagoras. 3 Upon their joining the covering force the Macedonians, having received such a large reinforcement, pressed hard on the enemy and in their turn began to drive the Romans from their heights. 4 But the chief obstacle to their putting the enemy entirely to rout was the high spirit of the Aetolian cavalry who fought with desperate gallantry. 5 For as much as the Aetolian infantry is inferior in the equipment and discipline required for a general engagement, by so much

N – Tarentine and Campanian Hoplites

The Roman Republic could trust his Italic allies, such as Etruscans and Latins. However, the recently conquered Samnites, Bruttians, and Campanians, as well as the Greek cities of Southern Italy and Sicily were less trustworthy. Thus Capua, Tarentum, and most notably Syracuse deserted to Hannibal in the wake of Cannae.

The figure on the left depicts a Tarentine hoplite. Dressed in a red tunic and sandals, he sports a defensive armament common to the Greek city states, the *linothorax*, or the linen corselet, ending in a row of *pteryges*, greaves, and a Chalcidian helmet, topped by a horse crest. He is defended by a wide round shield, the *hoplon*. The Chalcidian helmet developed from the well-known Corinthian helmet. This was a bronze helmet, covering the head and neck, sporting slits for the eyes and mouth, and a special cover for the nose. The main disadvantage was that it was impossible to hear anything. Thus, the Chalcidian helmet was a later variation, which left the mouth and ears clear, sporting hinged cheek pieces. The large round shield is quite similar to a much earlier shields, albeit in wood, covered by a bronze facing, such as an Etruscan shield in Vatican Museum. Often, as in this case, the *hoplon* was made only in wood, lined on the inside with leather. The *hoplon* had a slightly convex shape and was characterized by a large edge. A buttressing plate was often secured on the inside. An armband stood in the center of the shield, while, near the rim, was fixed a handgrip. The outer part of the shield was decorated with a heraldic motive, often painted.

The figure on the right depicts a Campanian hoplite. He is dressed in a blue tunic and sandals. He wears on his head an Etrusco-Corinthian helmet with cheekpieces, a central elevated crest of horse hair as well as two feathers on the side. He is defended by a bronze *cardiophylax*, a breastplate and backplate in bronze, covering the central part of the abdomen, shaped like a muscled cuirass and a bronze belt. When he was not fighting, the hoplite could wear the helmet, inclined upward, for ease. Later on, in Italy was produced a variant. This was shaped as the traditional Corinthian helmet but it was worn as a hat. Its main characteristic was that the slits for the eyes were almost closed, and later on in relief. Later check pieces, as in this case, were added. While triple disc breastplates were associated to Samnites, Campanians used larger square breastplates. These cuirasses had shoulder plates as well as side plates, usually hinged to the back plate. The anatomical decoration was influenced by the Greek muscled cuirass. Sometimes bronze muscled cuirasses were used as well. The broad bronze belt, which covered the navel, was a symbol of manhood. The main weapon used by the hoplite was the spear, often 2-3 m long. Greek spears are characterized by bronze leaf-shaped blades and metal spikes, at the butt end. The sword, less used, was a straight *xiphos*, with a leaf shaped blade about 60 cm long, or the curved *kopis*.

is their cavalry superior to that of other Greeks in detached and single combats. 6 Thus on the present occasion they so far checked the spirit of the enemy's advance that the Romans were not as before driven down to the level ground, but when they were at a short distance from it turned and steadied themselves. 7 Flamininus, upon seeing that not only had his light infantry and cavalry given way, but that his whole army was flustered owing to this, led out all his forces and drew them up in order of battle close to the hills. 8 At the same time one messenger after another from the covering force came running to Philip shouting, "Sire, the enemy are flying: do not lose the opportunity: the barbarians cannot stand before us: the day is yours now: this is your time"; 9 so that Philip, though he was not satisfied with the ground, still allowed himself to be provoked to do battle. The above-mentioned hills are, I should say, called "The Dog's Heads" (Cynoscephalae): they are very rough and broken and attain a considerable height. 10 Philip, therefore, foreseeing what difficulties the ground would present, was at first by no means disposed to fight, but now urged on by these excessively sanguine reports he ordered his army to be led out of the entrenched camp. 23 1 Flamininus, having drawn up his whole army in line, both took steps to cover the retreat of his advanced force and walking along the ranks addressed his men. 2 His address was brief, but vivid and easily understood by his hearers. For pointing to the enemy, who were now in full view, he said to his men, 3 "Are these not the Macedonians whom, when they held the pass leading to Eordaea, you under Sulpicius attacked in the open and forced to retreat to the higher ground after slaying many of them? 4 Are these not the same Macedonians who when they held that desperately difficult position in Epirus you compelled by your valour to throw away their shields and take to flight, never stopping until they got home to Macedonia? 5 What reason, then, have you to be timid now when you are about to do battle with the same men on equal terms? What need for you to dread a recurrence of former danger, when you should rather on the contrary derive confidence from memory of the past! 6 And so, my men, encouraging each other dash onto the fray and put forth all your strength. For if it be the will of Heaven, I feel sure that this battle will end like the former ones." 7 After speaking thus he ordered those on the right to remain where they were with the elephants in front of them, and taking with him the left half of the army, advanced to meet the enemy in imposing style. 8 The advanced force of the Romans thus supported by the infantry of the legions now turned and fell upon their foes. 24 1 Philip at this time, now that he saw the greater part of his army drawn up outside the entrenchment, advanced with the *peltasts* and the right wing of phalanx, ascending energetically the slope that led to the hills 2 and giving orders to Nicanor, who was nicknamed the elephant, to see that the rest of his army followed him at once. 3 When the leading ranks reached the top of the pass, he wheeled to the left, and occupied the summits above it; for, as the Macedonian advanced force had pressed the Romans for a considerable distance down the opposite side of the hills, he found these summits abandoned. 4 While he was still deploying his force on the right his mercenaries appeared hotly pursued by the Romans. 5 For when the heavy-armed Roman infantry had joined the light infantry, as I said, and gave them their support in the battle, they availed themselves of the additional weight thus thrown into the scale, and pressing heavily on the enemy killed many of them. 6 When the king, just after his arrival, saw that the light infantry were engaged not far from the hostile camp he was overjoyed, but now on seeing his own men giving way in their turn and in urgent need of support, he was compelled to go to their assistance and thus decide the whole fate of the army on the spur of the moment, although the greater portion of the phalanx was still on the march and approaching the hills. 8 Receiving those who were engaged with the enemy, he placed them all, both foot and horse, on his right wing and ordered the *peltasts* and that part of the phalanx he had with him to double their depth and close up towards the right. 9 Upon this being done, the enemy being now close upon them, orders were sent out to the men of the phalanx to lower their spears and charge, while the light infantry were ordered to place themselves on the flank. 10 At the same moment Flamininus, having received his advanced force into the gaps between the maniples, fell upon the enemy. 25 1 As the encounter of the two armies was accompanied by deafening shouts and cries, both of them uttering their war-cry and those outside the battle also cheering the combatants, the spectacle was such as to inspire terror and acute anxiety. 2 Philip's right wing acquitted themselves splendidly in the battle, as they were charging from higher ground and were superior in the weight of their formation, the nature of their arms also giving them a decided advantage on the present occasion. 3 But as for the rest of his army, those next to the force actually engaged were still at a distance from the enemy and those on the left had only just surmounted the ridge and come into view of the summits. 4 Flamininus, seeing that his men could not sustain the charge of the phalanx, but that since his left was being forced back, some of them having already perished and others retreating slowly, his only hope of safety lay in his right, hastened to place himself in command there, 5 and observing that those of the enemy who were next the actual combatants were idle, and that some of the rest were still descending to meet him from the summits and others had halted on the heights, placed his elephants in front and led on his legions to the attack. 6 The Macedonians now, having no one to give them orders and being unable to adopt the formation proper to the phalanx, in part owing to the difficulty of the ground and in part because they were trying to reach the combatants and were still in marching order and not in line, 7 did not even wait until they were at close quarters with the Romans, but gave way thrown into confusion and broken up by the elephants alone. 26 1 Most of the Romans followed up these fugitives and continued to put them to the sword: but one of the tribunes with them, taking not more than twenty maniples and judging on the spur of the moment what ought to be done, contributed much to the total victory. 3 For noticing that the Macedonians under Philip had advanced a long way in front of the rest, and were by their weight forcing back the Roman left, he quitted those on the right, who were now clearly victorious, and wheeling his force in the direction of the scene of combat and thus getting behind the Macedonians, he fell upon them in the rear. 4 As it is impossible for the phalanx to turn right about face or to fight man to man, he now pressed his attack home, killing those he found in his way, who were incapable of protecting themselves, until the whole Macedonian force were compelled to throw away their shields and take to flight, attacked now also by the troops who had yielded before their frontal charge and who now turned and faced them. 6 Philip at first, as I said, judging from the success of those under his own leadership, was convinced that his victory was complete, 7 but now on suddenly seeing that the Macedonians were throwing away their shields and that the enemy had attacked them in the rear, retired with a small number of horse and foot to a short distance from the scene of action and remained to observe the whole scene. 8 When he noticed that the Romans in pursuit of his left wing had already reached the summits, he decided to fly, collecting hastily as many Thracians and Macedonians as he could. 9 Flamininus, pursuing the fugitives and finding when he reached the crest of the ridge that the ranks of the Macedonian left were just attaining the summits, at first halted. 10 The enemy were now holding up their spears, as is the Macedonian custom when they either surrender or go over to the enemy, 11 and on learning the significance of this he kept back his men, thinking to spare the beaten force. 12 But while he was still making up his mind some of the Romans who had advanced further fell on them from above and began to cut them down. Most of them perished, a very few escaping after throwing away their shields. 27 1 The battle being now over and the Romans everywhere victorious, Philip retreated towards Tempe. 2 He spent the following night under canvas at a place called "Alexander's Tower" and next day went on to Gonni at the entrance of Tempe, and remained there wishing to pick up the survivors of the rout. 3 The Romans, after following up the fugitives for a certain distance, began, some of them, to strip the dead and others to collect prisoners, but most of them ran to plunder the enemy's camp. 4 Finding, however, that the Aetolians had anticipated them there and considering themselves defrauded of the booty that was rightfully theirs, they began to find fault with the Aetolians and told their general that he imposed the risk on them and gave up the booty to others. 5 For the present they returned to their own camp and

retired to rest, and spent the next day in collecting prisoners and what was left of the spoil and also in advancing in the direction of Larisa. 6 Of the Romans about seven hundred fell and the total Macedonian loss amounted to about eight thousand killed and not fewer than five thousand captured.7 Such was the result of the battle at Cynoscephalae between the Romans and Philip."[38]

"XXXIII.3. Philip, too, seeing that his ambassadors had brought from Rome no indication of peace, at the [2] beginning of spring decided to conduct a levy through all the towns of his kingdom, since he was in great want of young recruits. [3] For the continuous fighting through several generations had exhausted the Macedonians; during his own reign many had fallen in naval battles with the Rhodians and Attalus and in engagements with the Romans on land. [4] He therefore enlisted recruits from the age of sixteen, and some who had served their allotted time but still possessed some share of strength were recalled to the colours. He thus filled up his ranks, and ordered a muster of all his troops at Dium1 about the time of the vernal equinox. [5] There he established a base and spent the time of waiting for the enemy in drilling his troops daily. [6] Quinctius also meanwhile had left Elatia and marched to Thermopylae by way of Thronium and Scarphea. [7] There he held the Aetolian council, summoned to meet at Heraclea, to determine with how many troops they should follow the Romans to the war. [8] Having learned the decision of the allies, he advanced in three days from Heraclea to Xyniae, on the frontier of the Aenianes and Thessalians and made camp and waited for the Aetolian auxiliaries. These made haste, and six hundred infantry and four hundred cavalry arrived, commanded by Phaeneas. [9] Quinctius broke camp at once, so as to leave no doubt why he had waited. [10] When he had crossed the border into the Phthiotic country, five hundred Gortynii from Crete under the command of Cydas and three hundred from Apollonia, armed in the same fashion, joined him and a little later Amynander arrived with twelve hundred infantry of the Athamanes. Philip learned of the departure of the Romans from Elatia, and since he was in a situation where a contest for supreme power impended, he determined to encourage his troops. [11] After he had repeated many oft-told stories of the brave deeds of their forefathers [12] and also of the martial glory of the Macedonians, he came to the points which at that time were causing them the greatest terror and by which they could be roused to some degree of hopefulness. 4. Against the defeat sustained in the narrows at the Aous river he set the triple defeat

38   Polybius V, *Histories*, Books 16-27 (Translation of William R. Paton; Loeb Classical Library; Cambridge, Harvard University Press 2012).

O-P – *Macedonian Phalanx Advancing (see also pag.76)*

These two plates depict the Macedonian phalanx advancing. Most soldiers, dressed in a tunic and sandals, were defended by a *linothorax*, a helmet, often a Thracian, or Attic type, the *aspis*, or the round shield, and greaves. Their offensive weapons consisted in the long *sarissa* and the *xiphos*, or sword. The round shield, or aspis, is described by Plutarch, when he narrates the battle of Pydna. The shield was hung on the left shoulder. Once facing the enemy, the heavy infantrymen brought the aspis round to the front. The main reason that this rimless, slightly convex, round shield, similar to the *hoplon*, but quite smaller, was adopted, is that the *sarissa* was so long that the soldiers had to hold it with two hands. It was impractical to use the *sarissa*, while holding the hoplite shield. These shields are depicted everywhere, on the wall paintings of Macedonian tombs, such as the Tomb of Lyson and Kallikles, as well as the reliefs from the Temple of Athena at Pergamum, or those of the monument of Aemilius Paullus at Delphi. Besides, Macedonian shields were also depicted on coins. Inside, the shield was quite similar to the earlier *hoplon*, as it had a central armband, as well as a handgrip near the edge. The most common motives painted were the six, or eight-pointed star, possibly the dynastic emblem of the Macedonian monarchy, as well as symmetrical geometric patterns based on several crescent positioned around the circumference. Sometimes the star and the geometric patterns were combined together. Wreaths, as well as anchors, also could emblazon the shield. The *sarissa* was a long pike, hold in both hands, that could reach 5.5 m long. However, by the end of the third century BCE, according to Polybius, it could reach 6.5 m long. The *sarissa* had a bronze or iron head as well as a counter-weighted butt.

inflicted at Atrax by the Macedonian phalanx upon the Romans. [2] Even there, when they had failed to hold the passes of Epirus which they commanded, the blame rested first on those who had not maintained careful vigilance, next, in the actual battle, on the light infantry and the mercenaries; [3] the Macedonian phalanx, on the other hand, had stood fast even then, and would always stand unconquered when regular battle was joined on level ground. [4] There were sixteen thousand in the phalanx, the flower of the whole kingdom. In addition, there were two thousand with light shields, whom they call *peltasts*, and an equal number (two thousand each) of Thracians and Illyrians —Tralles [5] is the name of the tribe —and auxiliary mercenaries from different nationalities to the number of about fifteen hundred and two thousand cavalry. With these forces the king awaited the enemy. [6] The Romans had about the same number; it was only in cavalry strength that they were superior, because of the arrival of the Aetolians. 5. When Quinctius had moved his camp towards Phthiotic Thebes, he conceived the hope that the city would be betrayed to him by Timon, a leader among this people, and approached it with a few cavalry and light infantry. [2] This hope was so wholly belied that there was not only a battle with forces which sallied forth, but there was even grave danger had not infantry and cavalry, hastily summoned from the camp, arrived in time. [3] And after nothing of this rashly-formed hope turned out well, he gave up for the present his design of further attacks upon the town. [4] And, assured that the king was in Thessaly, but not yet certain of the direction of his march, he ordered soldiers sent out into the country to cut timbers and prepare a stockade.1 [5] Both Macedonians and Greeks employed a stockade, but in a manner ill adapted to ease of transportation or security in defence; [6] for they cut trees of too great size and with too many branches for one soldier to carry, especially with his arms, and when they had walled a camp by planting these in front, the destruction of their rampart was easy. [7] For because the trunks of the great trees were planted far apart and numerous strong branches offered easy holds for the hand, two or at most three young men, if they exerted themselves, would easily pull out a tree, and, [8] this being pulled out, there was at once an opening like a gate, nor was material ready at hand to block it. [9] The Roman cuts light forked trees with three or perhaps four branches, as a general rule, so that each soldier could comfortably carry several at once, with his arms hanging on his back; [10] and they plant them so close together and interweave the boughs so completely that it is difficult to tell to which branch each trunk is joined or to which trunk each branch belongs; [11] moreover, the branches are so sharp as to leave, interlaced, little space for inserting the hand, so that there is nothing that can be grasped and pulled out, since the interwoven branches bind one another together; [12] and, if one is by chance pulled out, it leaves a small gap and is easily replaced. 6. Quinctius made a short march the next day, the soldiers carrying the stockade with them, so that he was ready [2] to fortify a camp in any place, and when he had halted about six miles from Pherae, he sent out patrols to find out in what part of Thessaly the king was and what he was doing. [3] The king was near Larisa. Being now informed that the Roman had moved from Thebes to Pherae and desiring, for his part, to end the struggle at once, he began to march towards the enemy and encamped about four miles from Pherae. [4] Thence next day both sides sent out light troops to seize the hills overlooking the town, and these, when they were about equidistant from the ridge which was to be occupied, came to [5] a halt as soon as they espied one another, waiting quietly for the runners whom they had sent back to camp to ask what they were to do, since the enemy had unexpectedly been met. [6] And on that day indeed they were withdrawn to camp without starting a battle; on the next day there was a cavalry engagement around the same hills, in which, mainly through the help of the Aetolians, the king's forces were defeated and driven back to their camp. [7] Both sides were greatly hindered in the action by the fact that the country was covered with many trees and gardens, as in suburban districts, while the roads were bordered with hedges and in some places entirely closed. [8] Both commanders therefore reached the same decision, to retire from this country, and as if by agreement both marched in the direction of Scotusa, Philip hoping to find food there, the Roman by his advance to destroy the enemy's grain-supply. [9] The two columns marched the whole day, nowhere seeing one another, since there was a continuous range of hills between them. The Romans encamped near Eretria in Phthiotis, Philip on the river Onchestus. [10] Nor did either army know for certain where the [11] enemy was, even the following day, though Philip encamped near Melambium, as they call it, in the country of Scotusa, and the Romans around Thetideum, in the territory of Pharsalia. [12] The third day a heavy rain, followed by a fog dark as night, kept the Romans in camp in fear of an ambuscade. 7. Philip wished to hurry and so ordered an advance, undeterred by the low-hanging clouds after the rain; [2] but so dense a fog obscured the day that the standard-bearers could not see the road nor the soldiers the standards, and the column, straggling along in obedience to the various cries, was as disorderly as if wandering about at night. [3] They crossed the hills which are called Cynoscephalae and encamped after leaving there a strong guard of infantry and cavalry. [4] Although the Roman had stayed in the same camp near Thetideum, nevertheless he sent out ten troops of cavalry and one thousand infantry to discover where the enemy was, with orders to guard against ambushes, which the darkness would hide, even in open country. [5] When they came to the guarded hills, both forces remained passive, as if struck with a mutual fear; then they sent messengers back to the camps to their commanders, as soon as their panic from this unexpected contact had subsided, and did not longer postpone the fight. The battle began at first with skirmishes of a few scouts in advance, then assumed larger proportions as reinforcements came to the aid of the defeated. [6] In this battle, when the Romans were not holding their own, but kept sending message after message to their commander that they were hard pressed, five hundred cavalry and two thousand infantry, [7] mostly Aetolians, under two military tribunes, were speedily sent and restored the unfavorable battle, and as fortune changed the Macedonians, finding themselves in difficulties, begged through messengers for aid from the king. [8] But since he had expected anything but a pitched battle that day, on account of the general darkness from the fog, having sent most of his troops of every sort out to forage, he hesitated for a time, not knowing what to do; [9] then, as messengers kept urging him, and the fog had now uncovered the ridges of the mountains and he could see the Macedonians crowded together on the highest of a number of hills, defending themselves more with the advantage of position than with arms, thinking that he must at any [10] rate stake everything, lest he suffer the loss of some of his men, left unsupported, he sent Athenagoras, commander of the mercenaries, [11] with all the auxiliaries except the Thracians and with the Macedonian and Thessalian cavalry. [12] On their arrival the Romans were driven from the ridge and checked their retreat only when they reached more level ground in the valley. The Aetolian cavalry was the greatest safeguard to prevent their utter rout. [13] At that time their cavalry was by far the best in Greece; in infantry they were inferior to their neighbours. 8. The news was more encouraging than their success in the battle warranted, since one after another, coming back from the field, shouted out that the Romans were fleeing in terror, and [2] this compelled Philip, though against his will, reluctant, and maintaining that it was a rash undertaking and that he liked neither the place nor the time, to commit his entire force to the action. [3] The Roman also did the same, from necessity rather than to seize an opportunity for fighting. The right wing, with the elephants alined in front of the standards, he held in reserve; [4] with the left and all the lightarmed troops he attacked the enemy, reminding them at the same time that they would meet the same Macedonians whom they had driven out and defeated in battle in the passes of Epirus, defended by mountains and rivers, conquering the difficulties of Nature herself, the same Macedonians whom they had previously defeated under the leadership of Publius Sulpicius, when they held the pass to Eordaea; [5] that the Macedonian kingdom rested on reputation and not on strength, and that even this reputation had at last wholly faded away. [6] By this time they had come up to their men stationed in the lowest part of the valley, who, encouraged by the arrival of the army and the general, renewed the battle, charged, and again drove back the enemy. [7] Philip with the *peltasts* and the right wing of the infantry, the strength of the Macedonian army, which they called the phalanx, advanced on the run to meet the enemy, ordering Nicanor, one of [8] his nobles, to follow at once with the rest of the army. [9] At first as he reached the ridge and saw

that the battle was over there, with a few weapons and a few corpses of the enemy lying about, and that the Romans had been driven back from there and that the battle was raging near the enemy's camp, he was filled with excessive joy; [10] presently, as his men were retreating, made uncertain by the reversal of fear, he debated in terror whether he should withdraw his men to their own camp; [11] then, as the enemy came nearer, when his men were being cut down in flight and could not be rescued unless they were reinforced, and not even he had any safe line of retreat, he was compelled, though his whole force had not come up, to try desperate measures. [12] On the right flank he placed the cavalry and the light infantry who had been in the battle; [13] he ordered the *peltasts* and the Macedonian phalanx to put aside their spears, the length of which was a hindrance, and to engage with swords. [14] At the same time, to prevent the line from being easily broken through, he diminished the front by half and doubled the depth by extending the files backward, so that the formation was deep rather than wide; he also ordered the troops to lessen intervals, so that man stood close to man and arms to arms. 9. Quinctius absorbed into his ranks and among₁ the standards the men who had already been engaged and gave the signal with the trumpet. [2] They say that only rarely at any other time has such a shout been raised at the beginning of a battle, for, as it happened, both armies shouted at once, and not only those who were fighting but also the reserves and those who were just then coming up to the line. [3] On the right flank, the king prevailed easily, mainly because of his position, since he was fighting from higher ground; on the left there was panic and confusion, especially since the part of the phalanx which was in the rear was still coming up; [4] the centre, which was nearer the right flank, stood watching the battle there, as if it were a spectacle which did not directly concern them. [5] The phalanx, which had come up in column rather than in line, and in a form more fitted for the march than for battle, had barely reached the saddle. [6] While it was still in disorder, Quinctius, although he saw his men retreating on the right, first sending his elephants against the enemy, attacked, thinking that the defeat of a part would involve the rest. The issue was never in doubt; the Macedonians immediately fled, turning back in terror at the first sight of the beasts. [7] The others too followed them in their flight, and one of the tribunes [8] of the soldiers, forming a plan to fit the emergency, took the soldiers of twenty companies and, leaving the action where his men were clearly victorious and making a short detour, attacked the enemy's right from behind. [9] Any army would have been dismayed by an attack from the rear; but added to the general panic of all in such a crisis was the fact that the heavy and unwieldy Macedonian phalanx could not change front, nor did the soldiers who were falling back a little while before from the front upon men who were by now terrified on their own account permit this. [10] They were at a disadvantage too because of their position, since the ridge from which they had been fighting, when they were pursuing the soldiers who had been driven down the hill, had been given up to the enemy which had been led around behind them. [11] For a while they were caught between the two lines and slaughtered, then most of them threw away their arms and took to flight. 10. Philip with a few troopers and infantrymen at first held a hill higher than the rest, so as to watch the fortune of his left flank; [2] later, when he beheld the disorderly flight and saw all the ridges round about filled with the gleam of standards and arms, he too left the field. [3] Quinctius, after pressing hard on the retreating enemy, suddenly, because he saw the Macedonians raising their spears, and not knowing what this meant, halted his troops for a moment because of the strangeness of the action. [4] Then, when he learned that it was the customary gesture of the Macedonians to indicate their surrender, it was in his mind to spare the vanquished. [5] But the soldiers, ignorant that the fighting was over, so far as the enemy was concerned, and not knowing the general's plans, charged, and killing the first put the rest to flight. [6] The king fled at full speed to Tempe. Then he stopped a day at Gonni to collect any who had survived from the battle. The victorious Romans burst into the enemy's camp in the hope of loot, but found that it₁ had, for the most part, already been plundered by the Aetolians. [7] On that day eight thousand of the enemy perished, five thousand were captured. [8] Of the victors about seven hundred fell. If we trust Valerius Antias, who is prone to increase numbers without restraint, forty thousand of the enemy were slain that day; the prisoners, he says —here his exaggeration is more moderate —numbered five thousand seven hundred, and two hundred and forty-nine standards were taken. [9] Claudius too gives the figures as thirty-two thousand killed and four thousand three hundred captured. [10] I have given my account, not because the numbers are smallest, but because I have followed Polybius, an authority worthy of credence on all matters of Roman history and especially on occurrences in Greece."[39]

In the aftermath of the victory, first negotiations were held in the Vale of Tempe between the Antigonid sovereign and Flamininus, who represented the Roman Republic. It was decided that the Macedonians would withdraw from Greece, Thrace, and Asia Minor. The peace treaty with Philip V, which followed put an end to the war. The most important clause of the treaty was that Philip V had to retire his garrisons from Greece, Thrace, and Asia Minor, to surrender his warships, as well as to pay a war indemnity of a thousand talents to Rome in installments extending for the period of ten years. Besides, the Greek cities and *ethne*, previously subjects to the power of Macedonia, were to be set free. The treaty ended in a declaration of friendship of *philia* between the victor, the Romans, and Philip, the defeated. Philip did not dare anymore to defy Roman power. During the Isthmian Games in 196 BCE, Titus Quinctius Flamininus proclaimed the liberty of Greece. After Cynoscephalae the history of the Cannae legions is unknown. What happened to these legions? They came back home? They finally settled?

Yet, the way to the Hellenistic East and to the Roman rule of the *oikoumenè* had been paved. The *legions cannenses* had made it possible.

---

39   Livy IX, *The History of Rome, Books 31-34* (Translation of Evan T. Sage; Loeb Classical Library; Cambridge, Harvard University Press 1935).

▲ **Coins minted by Philip V of Macedonia – *Tetradrachm***
Silver, minted 221-179 BC Obverse: Head of Philip V left, as the hero Perseus, lightly bearded and with a harpa over his right shoulder, wearing a winged helmet adorned with a griffin as a crest; all within the tondo of a Macedonia shield ornamented with seven stars within crescents around the edge. Reverse: Club to right; one monogram above and two below; all within oak wreath tied at the left; to left of the ties, kerykeion. Inscription ΒΑΣΙΛΕΩΣ ΦΙΛΙΠΠΟΥ, of King Philip.

CONCLUSIONS

The *legions cannenses* were the first professional army in the history of the Roman Republic. The *legiones cannenses* are indeed the first example in Roman history of a professional unit that served together with the other legions that were all units made of citizens. The *legiones cannenses* presented all the elements found in the later professional army of the Late Republic and Early Empire. First of all, these soldiers were separated from civic life. Second, the *legiones cannenses* were first of all more bounded to their commanders not to the Roman state. This bond was consolidated mainly with Scipio who gave to his veterans' land allotments strengthening the relationship *patronus - cliens*. Third, the tactic composition of the *legiones cannenses* evolved in a tactic unit more similar to that of the Roman legions after Marius. Fourth, once the tactic composition soldiers felt unsatisfied, they mutinied, once more a behavior typical of the late Republic and early Empire Roman legions.

However, there is a further reason, to evaluate as primary the role of the *legions cannenses* in the Second Punic War and in its aftermath, once considering quality versus quantity. According to Lazenby, the main reason for Rome's victory in the Second Punic War was its huge pool of manpower. Thus, in 218 BCE, on a total population of 325.000 m male adults, the Roman army could field 240.000 men.[40] Yet, the total number of Roman citizens who fought in the *legiones cannenses* did not reach more than 10.000 individuals. Although the total number of the soldiers who fought in the *legiones cannenses* was negligible, once compared to the manpower which the Roman Republic could field, yet, it is clear that their contribution to the final victory was probably crucial, as these were the first professional soldiers in the story of Rome.

Last but not least, the *legiones cannenses* were not the only example of the Pre Marian-professionalization of the army. Gabba shows that during the Second Punic War the enrolment of both the *capitecenses* or *proletarii* and the volunteers can be can be seen as a foreshadowing of the professionalism of the Roman army. Gabba argues that during the Second Punic War the successive reduction of the original Servian census of the rating of the fifth class bring to a proletarianization of the Roman city militia. The minimum census qualification decreased dramatically during the Second Punic War. Thus, in Servian Constitution the census qualification of fifth class was less than 11.000 asses (Livy, *History of Rome* I, 43), but Polybius reports that during the Second Punic war 4000 asses was the minimum census qualification for the fifth class (Polybius, *Histories* VI, 19, 2). This decrease of census qualification for fifth class was introduced in 214 BCE, and its original purpose was to obtain the sailors necessary to man the fleet. Besides, the introduction of the *velites* in the Roman Army was one of the consequences of the decrease of census qualification for fifth class (Livy, *History of Rome* XXVI, 4, 9). Moreover, Gabba emphasizes that during the Second Punic War for the first time appeared voluntary enlistment "en masse ".[41]

---

40   See A. F Lazenby, *Hannibal's War, A Military History of the Second Punic War*, Warminster 1978, pp. 234-235.
41   See Gabba, *Republican Rome, The Army and the Allies*, pp 1-2, 4-5, 11.

2

1

APPENDIX I

Total of the legions levied in the Second Punic War in A.J. Toynbee, *Hannibal's Legacy, The Hannibal War's effects on Roman Life, Rome and her Neighbours after Hannibal's exit*, London 1965, p. 647.

Year	Toynbee
218	6
217	11/13
216	17/13
215	14
214	20
213	22
212	25
211	23
210	21
209	21
208	21
207	23
206	20
205	18
204	19
203	20
202	16
201	15

Q – Advancing Macedonian Heavy Infantry

These five figures depict Macedonian heavy infantrymen, members of the Antigonid phalanx. Their defensive equipment is similar, but not identical. The iron or bronze helmets are of the Thracian or Attic type. Besides they all wear a cuirass, often the linen corselet, the *linothorax*, sometimes reinforced with metal plates, as well as muscled cuirasses. They all carry the *aspis*, the round shield. Greaves hold with straps complete their equipment. The Thracian helmet was characterized by a peak at the front and long pointed check pieces. These helmets were sometimes decorated with beard and moustaches, and cut away at the mouth and eyes. They could have an elongated shape, reproducing a Phrygian hat, or a simpler round cap, topped by a crest. The *linothorax*, or linen cuirass, which first appear in the Mycenean period, was adopted as the main, and most effective, body protection by the hoplites in the sixth century BCE. By the third century, most of the heavy infantry, who made up the phalanx had adopted the *linothorax*. An inscription from Amphipolis in Macedonia records that file leaders were fined twice as much as the other ranks for the loss of a cuirass. Evidently the front-rank men were defended by muscled cuirasses, or reinforced linen corselets. The *linothorax* was made of many layers of linen glued together to form a stiff blouse, half a centimeter thick. The lower part has cuts to make it easier to lean down. These slits were covered with a further layer of stripes, similarly cut, the *pteryges*, covering the gaps lefty by the inner layer. The cuirass was tied together to the left side. A U-shaped piece, fixed to the back, was drawn forward to cover the shoulders. By the Hellenistic period as attested in various paintings, such as the Tomb of Lyson and Kallikles, various painted stelae, coming from Macedonia or Alexandria, the *linothorax* by now had two superimposed rows of *pteryges*. Besides, shorter *pteryges* cover the upper parts of the arms. Scales, plates, or lamellar plates were all used to improve the protection.

APPENDIX II

The Roman Army from the Beginning of the Second Punic War to the end of 216

Year	De Sanctis	Connolly
218	6 legions: 1, 2, 3, 4 (Gallia), 5, 6 (Spain)	6 legions: 1 (levied in the preceding year), 2 - levied by Scipio to Gallia), 3, 4 (Longus – Gallia), 5, 6 (Publius Scipius /Cneus Scipio-Spain).
217 before Trasimenus	11 legions: 1, 2 (Gallia), 3, 4 (Etruria), 5, 6 (Spain), 7, 8 (Sicily), 9 (Sardinia), 10, 11 (Rome)	13 legions: 1, 2, 12, 13 (Geminus), 5, 6 (Spain – Scipiones), 3, 4, 10, 11 (Flaminius), 7, 8 (Sicily), 9 (Sardinia).
217 after Trasimenus	13 legions: 1, 2, 12, 13 (Lucania and Bruttium), 5, 6 (Spain), 7, 8 (Sicily), 9 (Sardinia), 10, 11 (Rome). 3+, 4+ (Etruria– destroyed at Trasimene).	13 legions: 1, 2, 12, 13, 14, 15, 16, 17 (Campania/ Apulia - Fabius Maximus and Minucius Rufus), 5, 6 (Spain – Scipiones), 7, 8 (Sicily), 9 (Sardinia).
216 before Cannae	17 legions: 5, 6 (Spain), 7, 8 (Sicily), 9 (Sardinia), 10+, 11+ (Gallia - destroyed by Celts), 14, 15 (Roma), 1+, 2+, 12+, 13+, (Apulia - destroyed at Cannae)	16/7 legions: 1, 2, 12, 13, 14, 15, 16, 17 (Aemilius Paulus and Terentio Varro - legions at Cannae), 18, 19 (Gallia under Postumus destroyed by Celts), 20, 21 (Roma – urbanae), 5, 6 (Spain – Scipiones), 7, 8 (Sicily), 9 (Sardinia).
216 after Cannae	13 legions: 16, 17 (Roma), 14, 15, C, C, V, V (Campania), 5, 6 (Spain), 7, 8 (Sicily), 9 (Sardinia)	15 legions: 5, 6 (Spain – Scipiones), 7, 8 (Sicily), 9 (Sardinia), 22, 23 (Roma - urbanae), 20, 21, V, V, C, C, N (Campania).

C = Legio Cannensis, V = Volones, N = Legio Nautica

The Cannae Legions in Sicily and Africa according to De Sanctis, in A.J. Toynbee, *Hannibal's Legacy, The Hannibal War's effects on Roman Life, Rome and her Neighbours after Hannibal's exit,* London 1965, pp. 648-649).

Sicily
215 CC
214 CC
213 CC+16th and 17th
212 CC+16th and 17th
211 CC+16th and 17th
210 CC+16th and 17th
209 CC
208 CC
207 CC
206 CC
205 CC
204 CC/ 39th and 40th
Africa
204 CC
203 CC
202 CC
201 CC

APPENDIX III

Hellenistic Warfare

The fourth century was a revolutionary period for the development of Classic warfare. Epaminondas of Thebes, Iphicrates of Athens, and, then, Philip II of Macedonia reshaped the tactics of the heavy infantry. Besides, in this period, the tasks of the light infantry evolved considerably. Moreover, Philip II developed the heavy cavalry as a striking force. Thus, the army of Alexander the Great, was no more based only on units of heavy infantry, such as the hoplites of the Graeco-Persian wars, but it included also other arms, such as the cavalry and the light infantry. The military developments in Greece at the beginning of the fourth century BCE were not lost on the Roman Republic. Thus, the reforms of Camillus, following the defeat of Allia in 390 BCE, reflect the contemporary fashion in Greece. The Athenian Iphicrates was a *strategos*, or military commander, who successfully modified the weaponry and tasks of the hoplites, the heavy infantry, and of the *peltasts*, the light infantry. The hoplites were now more lightly armed. Their equipment included a smaller round shield, and instead of graves, high boots, the Iphikratides. The thrusting spear was now 3, 6 m long. Also, the equipment of the *peltast* changed, but the other way around. Thus, the *peltast* was equipped with a helmet, a short thrusting spear, together with the two javelins, and the shield, the *pelta*, became bigger. Iphicrates's *peltasts* could also function as heavy infantry. The heavy infantry of Philip II of Macedonia was the model for the later Hellenistic armies' heavy infantry. The ideal Macedonian phalanx is described by Asclepiodotus. The phalanx, 16.000 men circa, commanded by a *strategos*, was composed by 64 *syntagmata* or battalions of 256 men; 32 *syntagmata* formed a wing, or *keras*, commanded by a *kerarch*. The *syntagma* was composed by 16 files or *lochoi*, each of 16 men. Each *lochos* was commanded by a *lochagos*. The back half *lochos* was commanded by the *ouragos*, the second in command, who stood at the back of the formation. *Lochoi* were coupled in pair, and were commanded by a *dilochites*. Four

▲ **Coins minted by Philip V of Macedonia – Tetradrachm**
Silver, Pella or Amphipolis mint, circa 220-211 BC. Obverse: Diademed head of Philip V right Reverse: Athena Alkidemos, seen from behind, advancing left, shield decorated with star on left arm, preparing to cast thunderbolt held aloft in right hand, ΣP monogram to inner left, EP monogram to inner right.

lochoi were commanded by a tetrarch. Eight *lochoi* were commanded by a *taxiarch*. The *syntagmatarch* commanded a *syntagma*. On the other hand, according to Aelianus the basic unit of the phalanx was the taxis, not the *syntagma*. The taxis, commanded by a *taxiarch*, was composed of three *lochoi*. The total strength of the taxis was 1536 men. A *lochos*, commanded by a *lochagos*, consisted in 32 *dekai*. The total strength of the *lochos* was 512 men. The *dekas*, which could number 10 – 16 men, was commanded by a *dekadarch*. Asclepiodotus describes also the organization of the Macedonian cavalry. The *hipparchia*, 1600 cavalrymen circa, was the standard unit. The *hipparchia* was divided in 8 squadrons or ilai, each of 200 men. The commander of an *ila* was the *ilarch*. On the other hand, according to Aelianus, the *hipparchia* was divided in two or three *ilai*, reaching a strength of 400-600 men. Besides, the *ile*, was divided in four *tetrarchiai* of 49 men commanded by a *tetrarch*. The Macedonian cavalry adopted a triangle shaped formation, while the allied Thessalian cavalry adopted generally a diamond shaped formation. This was the organization of the army of Alexander the Great.

The Hellenistic period oversaw various tactic developments. First of all, warfare became a science. Thus, various literary figures wrote about the art of warfare. First and foremost, the Achaean statesman Polybius of Megalopolis. As Polybius, most of those scholars were Stoic philosophers. Posidonius of Apamea (135 BCE-51 BCE) wrote a book dedicated to the *Art of Tactics*, now lost. He studied at Athens under Panetius. He also traveled widely. His most important book, now lost, is the *Histories* in 52 books, which continued the history of Polybius till the dictatorship of Sulla in 51 BCE. The *Art of Tactics*, also lost, was the base of Asclepiodotus, Aelianus and Arrian's Art of Tactics. Asclepiodotus, probably a disciple of Poseidonius, was also a Stoic philosopher. He wrote a book dedicated to tactics, which survived in part in Aelianus's book *Theory of Tactics*.

A typical Hellenistic army at the beginning of the second century BCE would be composed of various units. It would now include a guard, usually composed of crack regiments of all the arms represented in the army. The heavy infantry was still armed and organized as Philip II's Macedonian phalanx. On the other hand, a newly developed unit was that of the *thureophoroi* or heavy armed light infantry. Both the phalanx and the *thureophoroi* supported the bulk of the attack against the enemy infantries. The *thureophoros* appears in the second century BCE. He was armed as a *pelta*st (helmet, two javelins, and a thrusting spear), but instead of the *pelta*, he was equipped with a heavier shield called *thureos*, the oval Celtic shield, similar to the Roman scutum. The *thureophoroi* could be used as light as well as heavy infantry. The light infantry was composed of various units, such as slingers, archers, and javelin throwers. Although in most of the late Hellenistic armies, the light infantry was organized similarly to the heavy infantry, however, in the Seleucid army, the light infantry possessed an organization akin to that of the Roman army. Asclepiodotus describe the ideal formation of light infantry in the late Seleucid army. This unit, the *psilagia*, was molded on Roman units. The *psilagia*, which numbered 256 men, was divided in 2 *hekatontarchiai*. The *hekatontarchia*, 128 men, was divided in 2 *pentekontarchiai*. The *pentekontarchia*, which numbered 64 men, was divided in 2 *systaseis*. Each *systasis*, 32 men, was divided in 4 *lochoi*. The *lochos* numbered 8 men. Thus, the *psilagia* had the same strength of the Roman *manipulum*, while the *hekatontarchia* of the *centuria*. The light infantry would have served at the beginning of the battle to disorganize the enemy's heavier units. The cavalry would have included heavy cavalry, which was used to strike the enemy flanks or its back, and light cavalry, mainly with scouting tasks. Elephants also were now an integral part of the army, as well as artillery composed of various devices.

Following Rome's victorious campaigns, by the second half of the second century BCE, around 168 BCE, the Seleucid ruler Antiochus IV Epiphanes, reorganized the heavy infantry, molding it on the Roman legion. Thus, according to Ascelepiodotus, the heavy infantry was divided in units, the *phalangarchia*, which numbered 4096 men, organized and equipped as a Roman manipular legion. The *phalangarchia* was divided in 2 *merarchiai*, each 2048 men, commanded by a *merarches*. Each *merarchia* was divided in two *chiliarchiai*, numbering each 1024 men. The *chiliarchia* was divided in two *pentakosiarchiai*, each numbering 512 men. A *pentakosiarchia* was divided in two *syntagmata*, for a total of 256 men. A *syntagma* was divided in two *taxeis* of 128 men. A *taxis* was divided in four *tetrachiai*, each numbering 64 men. A *tetrarchia* was divided in four *lochoi* of 16 men. The *syntagma* clearly corresponds to a *manipulum*, while the taxis corresponds to a double *centuria*. A *hemilochos* of 8 men parallels a *contubernium*. According to papyri also the Ptolemaic late heavy infantry units were probably organized on the model of the manipular legion, probably in the same period. The main problem is that the organization of the bigger tactical units is unknown. On the other hand, we know that the chiliarchia or syntaxis, which numbered 1536 men was divided in six *semeiai*. The *semeia*, which numbered 252 men, was divided in 2 *hekatontarchiai*. The *hekatontarchia* of 128 men, was divided in two *pentekontarchiai*. The *pentekontarchia* numbered 64 men. The *semeia* clearly corresponds to a *manipulum*, while the *hekatontarchia* to a *centuria*. Only the big armies as those of the Seleucid and Ptolemies would have fielded such quantities of various different arms. Smaller armies, such as that of Antigonid Macedonia were composed only of heavy and light infantry and a heavy cavalry. Most of the soldiers were mercenaries, and some of them fought according to their native traditions.

The armies of the Hellenistic monarchies could fluctuate between thousands and hundreds of thousands. Thus, Pergamum in 171 BCE could send to the Roman Republic only 6000 infantrymen and 1000 horsemen. Also, the Antigonid Kingdom of Macedonia could muster an army that was definitely smaller than those of Philip and Alexander or of its Seleucid and Ptolemaic counterparts. Philip V at Cynoscephalae could muster only 22.000 men. The armies of Ptolemaic Egypt and of Seleucid Syria, on the other hand, could reach the numbers of the Antigonid armies. Ptolemy I could muster already in 312 BCE at Gaza 18.000 infantrymen and 4000 cavalrymen. A hundred years later, Ptolemy IV could muster in 217 BCE at Raphia an army of 70.000 infantrymen, 56.000 of whom constituted the phalanx, 5000 cavalrymen, and 73 African elephants. Their antagonists, the Seleucids had a no less impressive army. Thus, Seleucus I could muster at Issus 20.000 infantrymen and 12.000 cavalrymen. Antiochus III had at Raphia 62.000 infantrymen, of whom 32.000 phalangists, 6000 cavalrymen and 102 Indian elephants. At Magnesia in 171 BCE Antiochus III could field 45000, maybe 58.000 infantrymen, 12.000 cavalrymen, and 54 Indian elephants. Also, against the Maccabees the Seleucid army have to be singled out for its huge numbers. Thus, at the battle of Emmaus in 168 BCE the Seleucid army could muster 40.000 infantrymen and 7000 cavalrymen, according to one version. According to another, no less than 20.000 infantrymen. Later on, Lysias in his first campaign in Judaea could muster 60.000 infantrymen and 5000 horsemen. Bacchides had at Elasa 20.000 infantrymen and 2000 cavalrymen. In the west, Carthage could muster in 255 BCE after the battle of Bagradas at the height of the First Punic War 12.000 (8000 citizens) infantrymen and 4000 (2000 citizens) cavalrymen. During the Second Punic War, Hannibal at the battle of the Trebbia in 218 BCE and at the Trasimenus in 217 BCE could muster an army of 38.000 infantrymen. Later on, at Cannae in 216 BCE Hannibal could muster 40.000 infantrymen and 10.000 cavalrymen. In 202 BCE at Zama Hannibal could muster only 40.000 infantrymen and 80 elephants. This time the Numidian cavalry fought on the side of the Romans.

BIBLIOGRAPHY

-Badian, E., *"The family and early career of T. Quinctius Flamininus"*, Journal of Roman Studies 61, 1971, pp. 102-111.

-Billows, R.A., *Antigonus the One-Eyed and the Creation of the Hellenistic State, Hellenistic Culture and Society*, Berkeley 1997.

-Briscoe, J., *"Flamininus and Roman Politics, 200-189 B. C."*, Latomus 31, 1972, pp. 22-53.

-Brizzi, G., *Annibale, come un autobiografia, Le vite*, Milano 1994.

-Brizzi, G., *Scipione ed Annibale. La guerra per salvare Roma*, Bari 2007.

-Brunt, P.A., *Italian Manpower*, Oxford 1971.

-Canestrelli,G., Asta, L., Liguori, S., *L'armée de Hannibal, hypothèse de reconstruction, Forum Hannibal pour la paix et l'investissement, Tunisie*, Mars 2018, Europantiqua-Res Bellica.

-Cassola, F., *I gruppi politici romani nel III secolo a. C.*, Roma 1962.

-Cassola, F., *La politica di Flaminino e gli Scipioni*, Labeo, 1960, pp. 105-130.

-Caven, B., *The Punic Wars*, London 1980.

-Connolly, P., *The Roman Army*, London 1976.

-Connolly, P., *The Greek Armies*, London 1977.

-Connolly, P., *Hannibal and the Enemies of Rome*, London 1978.

-Connolly, P., *Greece and Rome at War*, London 1981.

-Gabba, E., *Republican Rome, The Army and the Allies*, Berkeley 1976.

-Goldsworthy, A., *The Fall of Carthage, The Punic Wars 265-146 BC*, London 2003.

-Gruen, E., *The Hellenistic World and the Coming of Rome II*, Berkeley 1984.

-Head, D., *Armies of the Macedonian and Punic Wars, 359 BC to 146 BC*, Goring-by-Sea 1982.

-Lazenby, A. F., *Hannibal's War, A Military History of the Second Punic War*, Warminster 1978.

-Lucchetti M. *L'esercito romano da Romolo a re Artù 3 vol.* Soldiershop Bergamo, 2013.

-Nicolet, C., *Le métier de citoyen dans la Rome républicaine*, Paris 1976.

-Nizza, D., *"Note sul vero luogo del nome della battaglia di Zama"*, Istituto Lombardo, Accademia di Scienze e Lettere 114, 1980, pp. 85-88.

-Salmon, E.T., *Roman Colonization under the Republic, Aspects of Greek and Roman Life*, London 1969.

-Scullard, H.H., *Scipio Africanus, Soldier and Politician*, London 1970.

-Sekunda, N., *The Ptolemaic Army*, Stockport 1994.

-Sekunda, N., *The Seleucid Army*, Stockport 1994.

-Toynbee, A.J., *Hannibal's Legacy, The Hannibal War's effects on Roman Life, Rome and her Neighbours after Hannibal's exit*, London 1965.

-Will, E., *Histoire politique du monde hellénistique, 323-30 av. J.-C.*, Paris 2003.

TITOLI PUBBLICATI - ALREADY PUBLISHING

SOLDIERS&WEAPONS 032

BRUNO MUGNAI - LUCA S. CRISTINI

L'ESERCITO IMPERIALE AL TEMPO DEL PRINCIPE EUGENIO DI SAVOIA 1690-1720. LA FANTERIA (3)

THE IMPERIAL ARMY IN THE AGE OF PRINCE EUGENE OF SAVOY - THE INFANTRY (3)

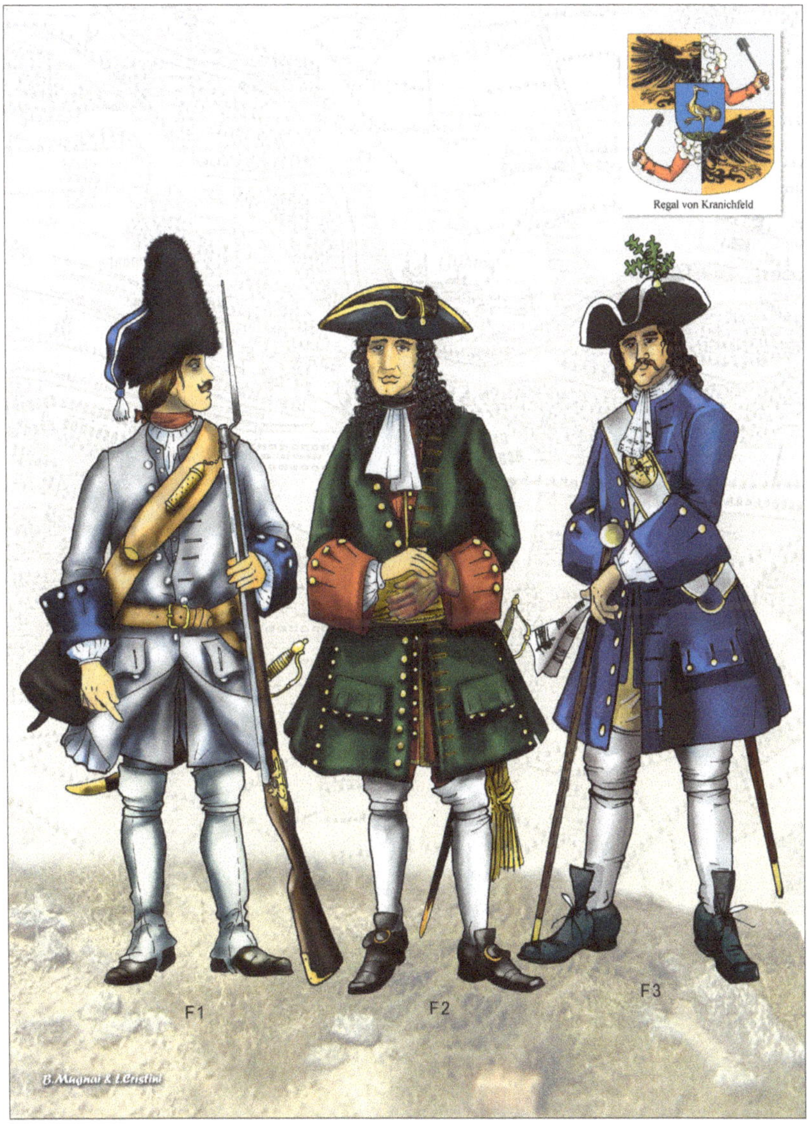

Regal von Kranichfeld

F1

F2

F3

B. Mugnai & L.Cristini

SOLDIERS&WEAPONS 003

AUTORI - AUTHORS:

Bruno Mugnai è nato a Firenze nel 1962 e ci vive con Silvia, Chiara ed Eugenio. Appassionato di storia militare fin da giovanissimo, ha pubblicato due libri sull'esercito ottomano dal 1645 al 1718; è inoltre autore di saggi sulle campagne italiane della guerra di Successione Spagnola e di articoli di uniformologia e storia militare del Seicento e del Settecento. Ha pubblicato per l'Ufficio Storico dell'esercito italiano una monografia sulle istituzioni militari dello stato di Lucca nell'Ottocento e per lo stesso editore ha completato un analogo contributo sull'esercito del granducato di Toscana dal 1737 al 1799. Con Luca Cristini ha collaborato alle illustrazioni dei due volumi dedicati alla guerra dei Trent'anni e alla realizzazione di diversi titoli della serie Soldiershop.

Luca Stefano Cristini, bergamasco, appassionato da sempre di storia militare. Dirige da diversi anni riviste nazionali specializzate di carattere storico uniformologico. Ha collaborato con l'editore Albertelli e De Agostini. Ha pubblicato un importante lavoro, su due tomi, dedicato alla guerra dei 30 anni (1618-1648) e uno studio in tre volumi sull'esercito imperiale nell'età di Eugenio di Savoia, scritto con B.Mugnai. Ha firmato molto titoli delle collane Soldiershop.

NOTE EDITORIALI - PUBLISHING'S NOTE

SOLDIERS&WEAPONS

La principale delle nostre collane di libri. Dedicata alla storia militare, alle uniformi e alle armi dei grandi eserciti del passato. Basata su testi di 68-80 pagine con diverse tavole a colori nelle pagine centrali e molte illustrazioni in b/n.

a Nonna Piera

ISBN: 978-88-9327-105-9   3rd edition: July 2016

Title: Soldiers&Weapons 003 - L'esercito Imperiale al tempo del Principe Eugenio di Savoia 1690-1720. La Fanteria (3) di Bruno Mugnai e Luca Stefano Cristini.
Editor: Soldiershop publishing. Cover & Art Design: Luca S. Cristini. Illustrazioni a colori di Bruno Mugnai e Luca Cristini.
.

In copertina : **Fanteria Imperiale 1715-1720**
Cover: Imperial infantry 1715-1720.